GOETHE & PALLADIO

Goethe's study of the relationship between art and nature,
leading through architecture to the discovery of
the metamorphosis of plants

DAVID LOWE / SIMON SHARP

Lindisfarne Books

copyright David Lowe and Simon Sharp 2005

Published by Lindisfarne Books
610 Main Street
Great Barrington, MA 01230

www.lindisfarne.org

LIBRARY OF CONGRESS CATALOGING-IN-PUBLICATION DATA

Lowe, David, 1950 Nov. 12-
  Goethe and Palladio Goethe's study of the relationship
between art and nature, leading through architecture to the discovery of the
metamorphosis of plants / David Lowe and Simon Sharp—1st ed.
     p. cm.
  Includes bibliographical references.
  ISBN 1-58420-036-7
  1. Goethe, Johann Wolfgang von, 1749-1832. Italienische
Reise. 2. Goethe, Johann Wolfgang von, 1749-1832—
Aesthetics.
  3. Palladio, Andrea, 1508-1580—Influence. 4. Nature
(Aesthetics) I. Sharp, Simon. II. Goethe, Johann Wolfgang von, 1749-1832.
Italienische Reise. English. Selections. III. Title.
PT2001.C4L69 2005
831'.6—dc22

10 9 8 7 6 5 4 3 2 1

Published in the United States of America

GOETHE & PALLADIO

Contents

List of Illustrations

Digest

The *Italian Journey* records an important part of Goethe's development as an artist and a scientist. It has two interweaving themes, Art and Nature. Goethe structured the account to show how through the working together of his experiences of art and nature in Italy a full understanding of metamorphosis developed in him.

The section of the *Italian Journey* that this study examines, from the Brenner Pass to Venice, shows that Goethe's interest in art is largely focused on the architecture of Palladio. The first chapter is an introduction to Goethe's relation to architecture with reference especially to an article by Nicholas Pevsner, the great architectural historian of the twentieth century.

The second chapter relates aspects of Goethe's life before his Italian journey, including his illnesses, his interest in alchemy and science, his activity as a freemason, and some of his literary works insofar as these are connected with his architectural interests in the first part of the journey. It ends with an examination of his aphoristic essay on Nature and his essay on Strasburg Minster.

In the third chapter, Goethe's statement that Palladio has shown him "the way to all art and life" is considered as an indication of the great extent to which Palladio affected him; and also in what way his experiences of Palladio's architecture contributed to his understanding of metamorphosis.

What has been argued for in the introduction—that the intention behind Goethe's reworking of his original journals and notes of the journey was to provide an account of his discovery of metamorphosis—is taken as an hypothesis in the fourth chapter to see what explanatory power such a viewpoint offers. The journey from the Brenner to Venice is examined in some detail to show how the polarity of art and nature is structured into it.

On the basis of this, the fifth chapter considers how Goethe's experiences of the architecture of Palladio affected his way of looking at both art and nature. Goethe's stated concern on the journey was to develop his way of seeing the world. The photographs in the appendix, which form an essential part of this project, attempt to interpret in a visual way not only which buildings of Palladio Goethe saw but also how he saw them. They are collected with quotations from Goethe in which he speaks of architecture, especially that of Palladio. (The original dissertation. was accompanied by a short video.) The photographs are largely ones that Simon took during the 10 months we spent following Goethe's *Italian Journey* day-by-day. Similarly many of the ideas expressed in this essay were born out of the conversations and experiences we had during that journey. We were particularly concerned as an artist and a writer to find a way of working together so that Goethe's ideas could come to life between us.

In the conclusion we examine the question raised by such a study as to the relationship between art and science and whether a Goethean way of looking at the phenomena of nature can also be applied to looking at art. The related question as to the relationship between sense-perception and imagination is implicit in much of the study. In this part of the *Italian Journey* Goethe points to the possibility of the forming of "exact sensory imaginations." The first he exemplifies is that of the locality of a plant or of a building; the second, that of considering the relationship of parts to the whole. The forming of these imaginations seems to be part of what Goethe developed on his journey to Italy through his experience of the architecture of Palladio. He later applied them in his search for the plant archetype and the metamorphosis sequence. Both these imaginations are particular to

Goethe's experiences in Italy. At the same time they are generally true for all things that have life. As such they may be seen to constitute a paradigm of a synthetic, *a priori* truth.

Appendix II has been added to what was in the original dissertation. It considers the insights Goethe gained during this part of his journey about the metamorphosis of plants and how these were related to his experiences of Palladio's work.

David Lowe and Simon Sharp,

OCTOBER 2005

CHAPTER 1

Introduction

In September, 1786 Goethe travelled south to Italy from the spa-town of Carlsbad where a few days earlier he had celebrated his thirty-seventh birthday. He reached Rome two months later in November, 1786. The following February he travelled further south to Naples and eventually to Sicily. He then had a second, longer stay in Rome, returning to Weimar in 1788.

The journey is generally seen as a crucial turning point in his biography. It was certainly central to his development as a writer, inaugurating his "classical" period, and has been much studied and commented upon.

Boyle in his biography explains Goethe's undertaking the journey as part of a wider social and cultural trend:

> There was also the belief that the places hallowed by ancient civilization and the physical remains of ancient art were the real objects to which the essential verbal and literary culture of northern Europe referred, that only if you came south of the Alps could all those Latin and Greek works become something more than abstract erudition.[1]

---

1. Boyle, N., *Goethe: The Poet and the Age, Volume 1*, Oxford University Press, 1991, p429.

Other writers have likened the idea of the classical world to a kind of memory image and a visit to Italy as a journey through time as much as space.[2]

Goethe himself experienced it as an artistic and moral metamorphosis. He writes in Rome:[3]

> I am like an architect who wants to raise a tower but has laid a poor foundation for it; he perceives that just in time and gladly pulls down what he has already erected, tries to expand and ennoble his plan, to become surer of his base, and rejoices beforehand in the more reliable solidity of the future edifice. May God grant that when I return, the moral consequence of having lived in a wider world will also be manifest in me. Yes, along with my artistic sense my moral one is undergoing a great renovation.

Indeed the writing down of what happened on the journey may be seen as an attempt to create a record of this change in the same way as he recorded the experiences of his early life in his autobiographical writings, *Poetry and Truth*.[4]

Interestingly, as Fink details in *Goethe's History of Science*,[5] it coincided too with Goethe's beginning to reissue his scientific writings as "notebooks." He included with them essays on how his scientific ideas developed. In relation to this, the *Italian Journey* could be seen as an autobiographical account of Goethe's discovery of metamorphosis, to which he attached great importance.

---

2. Although more concerned with a slightly earlier period, M.R. Lagerlof studies this aspect in *Ideal Landscapes*, Yale, 1990. See especially pp134-137.

3. *IJ*, December 20th. This and future quotations marked "IJ" are from J.W. von Goethe, *Italian Journey*. Translated by R.R. Heitner, Volume 6 in the collected works, published by Suhrkamp, New York: 1988.

4. Goethe, *From My Life: Poetry and Truth*, translated by R. R. Heitner and T.P. Saine. Volme 4 and 5 of the Suhrkamp Collected Edition, New York: 1984.

5. Fink, Karl J., *Goethe's History of Science*, Cambridge University Press, 1991, pp138-41.

Goethe wrote up his account of the journey from 1813 onwards, twenty-five years after he made the journey. Originally intended as a continuation of his autobiography, it was eventually published as the *Italian Journey* in two parts. The first part, to the end of the first Rome visit, was published in November, 1816 and the Naples and Sicily sections were published in October, 1817. The account of the second, longer stay in Rome did not appear until 1829.[6]

Because he made such a sustained effort on it, spanning sixteen years in his old age,[7] it was obviously something to which he attached some importance. It was based upon the journal and the letters he wrote on the journey,[8] though he altered these considerably.

It would be interesting to know what Goethe added later and what was written down on the journey. However, Goethe destroyed many letters and notes[9] so this is likely an impossible task. Despite the changes, Goethe is at pains, especially in the early part as far as the return to Rome from Sicily, to preserve the appearance of immediate experience[10] as though it were written on the spot.

The reader is invited to share in Goethe's experience, just as were the friends in Weimar to whom the original letters and journal were addressed. It is warm, thoughtful, speculative, often playful and humorous. It is also full of humanity and very approachable.

---

6. *IJ,*. Introduction, pp6,7.
7. Goethe was born in 1749 and died in 1832.
8. These are translated in *Flight to Italy* by Dr. T.J. Reed, Oxford University Press, 1999, hereafter referred to as *"Flight."*
9. See the article by Gerhard Schulz, *Goethe's Italienische Reise, especially pp 5&6*. In Hofmeister, G. et al, *Goethe in Italy*, Amsterdam: 1988.
10. Although it goes in a different direction than the one I wish to follow, Lagerlof in *Ideal Landscapes* has some interesting things to say about the rhetorical effect of presenting a memory as immediate experience. It is a theme taken up by other writers including Caroline van Eck in *Organicism in Nineteenth Century Architecture*, 1994. It leads into the literary rather than the visual experience of Goethe's Journey.

As one reads through it, following the journey, a theme becomes perceptible. At first it is in the background, inseparable from all the other incidental details being described. However, it gradually becomes clearer and more distinct so that the whole work takes on form. This theme runs through the entire journey and is developed in many different ways and in different contexts. It is first seen on the northern part of the journey. Here, as later in the journey, it is announced through two juxtaposed themes that weave in and out of the narrative pattern. These two poles of the journey are those of art and nature. This way of treating these two themes, like the North and South magnetic poles, or like positive and negative in electricity, already indicate Goethe's view of the relationship of art and nature.

As well as being vital to his development as a writer, this journey was also vital to Goethe's development as a scientist in that it led to his discovery of metamorphosis. Goethe's essay, *The Metamorphosis of Plants,* was written in the years immediately following his return from Italy. In other essays on the development of his botanical studies he clearly states that it owes much to his experiences in Italy.[11]

From this viewpoint, the *Italian Journey* is Goethe's record of his discovery of metamorphosis. His journey to Italy was the context, perhaps the necessary context, for the discovery, in so far as ideas that Goethe had been developing during the years preceding his journey were intensified and brought to realization in Italy.[12] The discovery is presented through his direct experience of nature on the journey. A good part of the narrative describes the landscape and scenery around him, talks about the formation of clouds, the kind of rocks he finds, and above all the plant life he sees.

Juxtaposed to these observations is the account of Goethe's experiences of art on the journey. These form the opposite pole of

---

11. Goethe, *The Author Relates the History of his Botanical Studies.* In *Goethe's Botanical Writings,* translated by Bertha Mueller, University of Hawaii, 1952.
12. *Flight,* p58.

the account and, at first glance, have less connection with his discovery of metamorphosis.

A significant feature of the *Italian Journey* is the amount of space that Goethe devotes to observations and thoughts about architecture. In the rest of his writings on art he gives more prominence to painting and sculpture. Studies of this aspect of the *Italian Journey* have generally emphasized his reaction to the architecture of Rome and the classical remains further south. Less attention has been paid to his architectural interests in the first part of the journey, passing through northern Italy across the plain of the Veneto, although there are in this first section many significant observations about the buildings he sees.

As the structure of the work became clearer to me, I noted the extent to which the references to architecture in this section focus on Palladio's architecture. This essay then concentrates on the effect of Palladio and his architecture on Goethe.

A useful summary of "Goethe and Architecture" is found in an essay of that name by Nicholas Pevsner. The first part of this examines Goethe's writings about Strasbourg Minster as exemplifying his changing relation to Gothic architecture in general and to that building in particular. It then moves on to consider the references in the Italian journey to architecture, focusing as others have done on Goethe's response to the ruins of Rome and then, further south, the Greek remains in Sicily and at Paestum,[13] Pevsner then remarks, almost as an aside: "From the very beginning and without any effort, he had been fascinated by Palladio." He continues, when speaking of Palladio in 1795 to "his friend and guide in artistic matters," Heinrich Meyer, to sum up his attitude: "The more one studies Palladio, the more incredible one finds the man's genius, mastery, richness, versatility and grace."[14]

---

13. A famous site of three Greek temples, south of Naples, which Goethe visited later in the journey.
14. Pevsner, *Goethe and Architecture*, in *Studies in Art, Architecture and Design*, London, 1968, p169.

The main thrust of Pevsner's article is to examine Goethe's relationship to Gothic architecture and how it was affected by his interest in classical architecture in Italy. The theme of this essay is rather with the effect of Palladio upon Goethe's Imagination.

Pevsner touches upon other themes which he does not develop but which have some relation to the subject of this project. I will therefore introduce them at this point. He quotes Goethe as saying,

> Classical, to me, means healthy, and romantic means sick.... Most of what is new is not romantic because it is new, but because it is weak and sickly and ailing. And what is old is not classical because it is old, but because it is strong, fresh, joyful and healthy.[15]

This represents a turning inside out of his pre-Italian-journey attitude toward the classical. Goethe had escaped from Weimar after a prolonged illness. It manifested in a curious way. He became ill whenever he had occasion even to look at a page of classical writing.[16] As we shall see, his interest in Palladio contributed to his recovery and the metamorphosis of his relation to what is classical.

A few lines after introducing this quote Pevsner, continuing his search for what Goethe means by "classical," mentions one of his maxims: "Those who have to borrow their proportions (what can be measured) from the ancients, must not complain, if we want to borrow from them what cannot be measured."[17] Pevsner relates this "something what cannot be measured" to the orders of architecture.

It may equally apply to something that, as a spatial form, appears through a temporal sequence. The plant archetype, in Goethe's sense, is such a spatial form that usually only comes to

---

15. Ibid., p171.
16. *IJ October 12*, p81. Goethe speaks about his illness at the end of the Venice section.
17. Pevsner, p171.

expression in the metamorphosis sequence, in time. The seed is planted in the ground. After some time the seed leaves, the cotyledons, appear. Later still, the leaves proper appear, and so on up to the formation of the new seed. The old seed and other parts of the sequence are by then no longer visible. This whole sequence is what Goethe presents as the plant archetype in *The Metamorphosis of Plants*.

For Palladio the orders are not just a measurable canon of proportions, no more than the metamorphosis sequence for Goethe is a scheme by which to analyze the stages of plant development. He writes: "Number and measurement in all their baldness destroy form and banish the spirit of living contemplation."[18]

Summerson in *The Classical Language of Architecture* speaks about Sir Edwin Lutyens' attitude to the orders. He did not believe that it was just a matter of imitation, of mere copying. At the same time you could not "play originality" with them. "They have to be so well digested that there is nothing but essence left. When right they are curiously lovely—unalterable as plant forms...."[19]

Even if Palladio's approach became a fixed set of Palladian rules to be followed, as Goethe points out, Palladio himself obviously felt free to break with a strict mathematical proportion and "put up the great picture he had in his mind even in places where it did not quite fit."[20] None of the actual columns he puts on his building are the "archetype" for the Corinthian order, the Ionic, etc., but they are right for that particular order. (Strictly speaking, in the Goethean sense, the archetype exists only for what has life.) Similarly, Goethe sees the metamorphosis sequence as something mobile. If you fix it down you move away from the archetype to the particular plant form.

---

18. Quoted in Naydler, J. *Goethe on Science*, Edinburgh: 1996, p66.
19. Sir Edwin Lutyens in a letter quoted but unfortunately not referenced by John Summerson, *The Classical Language of Architecture*, revised edition, 1980, p27.
20. *Flight*, p75.

When Goethe says there is something "godlike"[21] about Palladio's way of working, he refers to his understanding of the principles of his art. In his way of working he is like Nature who is consistent to the rules she follows even when she has to break them.[22] This may be an indication as to what Goethe refers to when he says that Palladio has given him "the way to all art and life."[23]

Pevsner seems to have some understanding of this connection, namely, that when you learn to look at what "cannot be measured" in architecture, you are looking at architecture in the same way as you are looking at a plant when you understand its connection with the plant archetype. Toward the end of his essay he quotes another passage by Goethe:

> In old German architecture, we see the flowering of a remarkable age. When one is confronted directly with such a flower one can only marvel at it; but if one looks into the innermost secret life of the plant, to see how it uses its strength and gradually unfolds, then one sees things with quite different eyes, and with understanding of what one sees.[24]

Pevsner prefaces it by saying the passage is "very important" and comments further:

> Thus Goethe's ideas about plant life, and about Gestaltung (morphology) and metamorphosis in general are here applied to architecture. It was an intellectual process, just like the process by which Goethe succeeded in appreciating the ruins of Paestum.[25]

---

21. *IJ September 19*, p47.
22. Goethe's Prose Poem to *Nature*, pp3-5, in *Goethe's Scientific Studies*, edited and translated by Douglas Miller, Volume 12 of the collected works, published by Suhrkamp, New York: 1988.
23. *IJ October 8*, p74.
24. Pevsner, p172.
25. Ibid.

Although Pevsner does not concern himself further with this thought of the connection between Goethe's ideas about plants and his ideas about architecture, he does feel that there is something important about it.

I agree with much of what Pevsner says, though I would want to characterize the "process" as an imaginative rather than an intellectual one. As Goethe says, it is "not measurable." When Goethe stands before the temples in Paestum he imagines himself back to the time when the temples were built, just as in the public gardens in Sicily when he sees the plant archetype for the first time he is, in imagination, in the time of the Homeric Greeks.

It is in fact this imaginative process that I am trying to uncover, the same process which can be applied to understanding the flowering of an artistic impulse as much as it can be applied to understanding why the rose flowers appear on the rose plant and the lily on the lily plant. I would emphasize: "One sees with quite different eyes and with understanding of what one sees."

This finds echoes in how Goethe speaks of his aim on the Italian journey, "Is my eye clear, pure and bright, how much can I grasp in passing, can the creases be eradicated that have formed and fixed themselves on my heart?" [26] In both cases learning how to see in a new way is connected with both architecture and plants.

I shall pursue this connection in what follows: first, by considering Goethe's relationship to art, especially architecture, before his Italian journey; second, to look at the stage of the journey from the Brenner Pass to Venice in some detail, and third to consider some methodological questions this study raises.

---

26. *IJ, September 11th*, p25.

CHAPTER 2

Imagination and the Senses

THE STORY OF Goethe's early life before the *Italian Journey* is found in his own autobiography[1] as well as in the many biographies, including the recent one by Nicholas Boyle.[2] I will examine his life insofar as to draw out certain themes which will contribute to a better understanding of the influence that Palladio and his architecture had on Goethe.

When Goethe left Karlsbad on September 3[rd,] he was fulfilling a long-held desire to see with his own eyes the country that he had heard so much about. His father had enjoyed his own journey to Italy and had brought back many souvenirs—cork models of buildings, paintings and drawings, models of gondolas and so on—which were in the house in Frankfurt where Goethe grew up. He encouraged his son to do a similar tour. The father too had written an account of his journey which in later life Goethe acquired.[3]

Goethe had learned to read Latin, Greek, Italian and other languages as a child. Through his reading of classical texts, Goethe had had around him, so to speak, images of the classical world.

1. Goethe, *From my Life: Poetry and Truth,* Volumes 4 and 5 of the Suhrkamp Collected Works.
2. Boyle, N. *Goethe: The Poet and the Age.*
3. Lange, V. *Goethe's Journey to Italy: The School of Seeing,* p147. In: Hoffmeister et al. *Goethe in Italy,* Amsterdam, 1988.

The mature Goethe, as dramatist, had a professional interest in the classical world. In 1779 he had written a version of the Greek play *Iphigenie in Tauris* for the court theatre in Weimar of which he was director. He played the male lead himself. He was, however, dissatisfied with it and when the question of its inclusion in his collected works came up, he decided to rewrite it. He took it with him to Italy and he was working on it intermittently during his journey through northern Italy. When Tischbein made his famous painting in Rome of *Goethe in the Campagna,* among the architectural fragment in the background he prominently displayed a relief depicting a scene from the play.

To say that Goethe had a long-held desire to see Italy was something of an understatement. In fact he tells us that the longing to see Italy was so strong that he could not even look at a classical text without becoming ill. In his letters to his friends in Weimar[4] he confesses this long-held secret and it is repeated in the account,[5] so we may take this as a genuine statement that the mere sight of the language of antiquity was enough to make him ill. The strength of this impulse that pushed him restlessly towards Rome culminated in the experience of his arrival in Rome as a "new birth,"[6] as a personal metamorphosis.

In the years in Weimar before his Italian journey, Goethe also started writing his two major literary works, *Wilhelm Meister* and *Faust.* In the figure of Mignon he brought to expression something of his hidden stream of longing for Italy. In *Wilhelm Meister's Theatrical Mission,* the early version of *Wilhelm Meister's Apprenticeship,* when Wilhelm asks this enigmatic androgynous figure about her origin, she replies with a song, *Kennst du das Land—Do you know the land where lemon trees bloom*—which articulates the separation of northern Europe from the sunny South.

---

4. *Flight,* p87.
5. *IJ, October12th,* p82.
6. *IJ, November1st,* p104.

"Know'st thou the house? Its ceilings columns bear the hall gleams white, its chambers shimmer fair, And marble statues, standing, gaze at me. ..."

"Italy must surely be meant," Wilhelm exclaims in response to her song. "Have you ever been to Italy?"

"Italy! If you go to Italy take me with you for here I freeze."[7]

Here the search for classical ground, which is referred to in the second verse of the song, is changed into something much more fundamental, something that life itself depends on.

Curiously, just before he reaches Innsbruck, near the Walchensee, Goethe meets a harper and his daughter on the road. In the novel, Mignon's destiny is strongly connected with that of an old harper who also plays a significant role in the novel. After another chance meeting, the next day Goethe comments, "Thus I meet my characters one by one."[8]

This search for Mignon's origins leads Wilhelm Goethe eventually to the architecture of Palladio. In Vicenza Goethe records that for a long time he was unsure whether to make Verona or Vicenza the home of Mignon. "Now I know," he writes, "it is Vicenza."[9]

Goethe felt the need to escape the rigor of his life in Weimar, for all its diversions and pleasures, in order to get back to the life of the artist.[10] For the journey he even changed his name and mostly preserved his incognito until he arrived in Naples. Though he did not give up writing, as Robson-Scott commented, "His energies were concentrated almost exclusively on the contemplation and practice of the visual arts." This statement by Robson-Scott must be qualified though by adding "... and looking

7. Goethe. *Wilhelm Meister's Theatrical Mission,* translated by G.A. Page, London: 1913, p172.

8. *IJ, September 8th*, p18

9. *Flight,* p49. See also, Streibel, A., *Goethe e Palladio* in Caputo, F. and Masiero, R. (eds) *Neoclassico,* Venezia, 1990, pp79-81.

10. Robson-Scott, W.D. *Goethe and the Visual Arts,* London: 1967, p4.

at and thinking about nature." The artistic side of Goethe is presented in *The Italian Journey* juxtaposed to his scientific interests.

The question of the relationship between imagination and sense perception is fundamental to understanding Goethe's way of seeing nature and art. Goethe's scientific approach developed from a deeply respectful, moral, even religious, feeling for nature. A consideration of this aspect of his response to nature will lead us on to an awareness of what, for a modern mind, seems an unusual aspect of Goethe's response to architecture.

Goethe, whether or not an alchemist, wrote with deep understanding of alchemy;[11] Faust after all is an alchemist. The play is full of events and symbols which require knowledge of alchemical and other occult sources to fully understand their meaning. After the serious illness in his eighteenth year, from which he nearly died, Goethe conducted alchemical experiments with Susanna von Klettenberg,[12] the leading light of the pietist circle to which his mother belonged.[13]

Shortly after Goethe came to Weimar he joined the Order of the Illuminati, to which the Duke and other members of the Court belonged. At the centre of their activity was the Dowager Duchess of Weimar, Anna Amalia, the mother of Karl August. Her summer residence at Tiefurt was the meeting place. Goethe was received into the Amalia Lodge of Freemasonry in Weimar as apprentice on June 23, 1781.[14] The following year, with due solemnities, he was raised to master.

There is every indication that Goethe was an active Freemason[15] though later on, with Karl August, he sought to suppress

---

11. Alchemy has a long history of development which extends as far back as the earliest written records of ancient China and continued in Europe well into the eighteenth century. *Goethe and Alchemy* is a thorough study of Goethe's knowledge of and interest in alchemy.
12. R.D. Grey, *Goethe the Alchemist*, Cambridge University Press, 1952, p4ff.
13. Goethe, *Poetry and Truth, part II, Book 8.*
14. Raphael, A. *Goethe's Parable*, New York: 1963, p63.
15. Curl, J.S. *Art and Architecture of Freemasonry*, London: 1991, p182.

the activity of the lodge. Again this may not be so much an indication of Goethe's opposition to an approach to life which gave prominence to its spiritual and moral aspects, but rather an indication that he was opposed to the corruption of the lodges and the scandal that came to surround them.[16]

The Amalia Lodge was closed for 26 years. However, during this time Goethe became a member of "Enge Bund," a small group that studied the history of Masonic symbolism. He assisted in the reorganization of the ritual and helped to create the one still in use.[17]

Many Masons such as Sandby and John Wood Senior, "who brought Palladianism to Bath, Bristol, and Liverpool" were respectable architects.[18] Wood believed the orders were divinely ordained and had first been used in Solomon's temple.[19] Indeed Freemasonry had its legendary origin in the building of Solomon's temple by Hiram Abiff.[20] Goethe as a Mason would be aware of this architectural connection since it was very much part of the ritual entry into the movement.

For Freemasons, architecture was "The Royal Art" and freemasonry was suffused with imagery drawn from the art of building. Equally, the architecture of Masons was often influenced quite openly by alchemical imagery. The memorial in Weimar to Goethe's friend and colleague, Herder, has the motto, "Light, Love, Life" within the frame, "of a serpent eating its tail: behind the serpent's head is a blazing sun, and in the centre of the circle are Alpha and Omega."[21] Herder was one of the first in the eighteenth

---

16. This was the time of the Cagliostro affair, and some Freemasons were involved in the excesses of the aftermath of the French Revolution. See Curl, p125.
17. Raphael, A. *Goethe's Parable,* New York: 1963, p63.
18. Curl, p91.
19. Curl, p91. Wood was also interested in Celtic prehistory. This influenced his work in Bath too. "The new city with its squares, terraces, crescents, forum, and circus was in fact a series of mystical symbols clothed in Classical Orders, that were not Greco-Roman but Divine."
20. Steiner, R. *The Temple Legend,* translated J.M. Wood, London: 1985, p73ff.
21. Curl, p124.

century to reach back beyond classical times and promote interest in Egyptian art and architecture. Alice Raphael's book *Goethe's Parable* contains much useful information about Goethe's relationship to Freemasonry. She suggests that the idea of Metamorphosis can be traced back to Alexandria and to Serapis, "the last of the Solar Gods." He was worshipped in Alexandria at the Serapeum, "a section of the city uniting East and West."[22] Here, as elsewhere, we can observe a process by which knowledge that had previously been held within the confines of the lodges and other closed circles was being spoken of more openly. This was the period in which Mozart was to write his opera, *The Magic Flute*.

In 1786, just before his journey, Goethe was lent a copy of *The Chymical Wedding of Christian Rosenkreutz*.[23] He read it and returned it to Charlotte von Stein[24] with a short note saying that there was a pretty fairy story in there but he did not have time to work on it. As *The Chymical Wedding* is fully immersed in the language and imagery of alchemy, it is interesting that the intended recipient of the original account of the *Italian Journey* was someone who shared Goethe's interest in it. The travel diary, on which the *Italian Journey* is based, was originally "a kind of long letter in installments to Frau von Stein."[25]

The fairy tale that Goethe suggests is in *The Chymical Wedding* was actually written down some eight years later in 1794. The Imaginations at work in *The Tale of the Green Snake and the Beautiful*

---

22. This was one of the architectural features rebuilt by the Emperor Hadrian in his villa at Tivoli.

23. An important alchemical text, supposedly written by Christian Rosenkreutz in 1459, circulated in the early 1600's.

24. Grey, p22 and p64.

25. Schulz, G. *Goethe's Italienische Reise*, p6. In: Hofmeister et al. *Goethe in Italy*. Schulz continues: "That the revisionary author of 30 years later should eliminate the most personal and intimate elements requires no particular explanation. Goethe's procedure was, however, dictated mainly by aesthetic considerations, so his revisions do not so much veil the past as raise it to the level of an autonomous work of art."

Lily[26] are clearly Goethe's, but they draw on Rosicrucian, Masonic and alchemical imagery.

The motifs of the underground temple, the three kings, the Old Man with the Lamp, the Lily and the Green Snake of the title indicate a continuation of his early interest in and involvement in such studies. Clear expression of this is given in such works as *"The Mysteries."*[27]

One of the incidental characters in *The Fairy Tale* is a pug dog called Mops. He is the pet of the Old Man with the lamp and his wife. In the course of the narrative he is turned to onyx. Although Goethe never offered an explanation of *The Fairy Tale*, it may be no accident that Goethe humorously appropriates the name of a prominent Masonic group. The name of the Society of the Mopses, "is taken from that of a pug or a young mastiff-type of dog with a pug-like face, noted for its courage and faithfulness. The order usually permitted women to all its offices except that of Grand Master."[28] Alice Raphael in her book about *The Tale of the Green Snake and the Beautiful Lily* suggests that this part of the story is based upon a Chinese Legend about Wei Po Yang, "the father of Chinese Alchemy." He made up a gold medicine and gave it to his little dog which caused its temporary death.[29]

As in *The Chymical Wedding,* the theme of sacrifice and renewal is central to the narrative of *The Fairy Tale*. In this sense the idea of metamorphosis is central to both the narrative of this story and to the *Chymical Wedding*. An imaginative connection to the metamorphosis sequence may also be seen in some of the details. The seven-day sequence of *The Chymical Wedding* is echoed in the seven stages of the Metamorphosis sequence. For example, on the first day Christian Rosenkreutz has a dream of

---

26. Goethe included this tale as part of *The Conversation of German Refugees,* included in Volume 10 of the Suhrkamp collected works, ed. J.K. Brown, translated by K. Winston et al. New York:1983.
27. Fragment of a poem, written 1784-6. See Boyle, p397.
28. Curl, p76.
29. Raphael, intro, pIX.

prisoners in a dark underground chamber being pulled up to the light. An obvious association is the plant being released from the seed and growing up to the surface. The parallels in *The Fairy Tale* are less clear, but much of the action of the story takes place in an underground temple which is eventually raised to the surface. In both of these works the motif of an underground or hidden temple is of importance to the transformation that occurs to the snake and to the beheaded kings and queens.

One of the four kings in the underground temple is made up of many different metals. Alice Raphael points out that, at the Serapeum in Alexandria where the god Serapis was worshipped, the colossal statue of Serapis was formed of all the metal conjoined "to symbolize the universe which is composed of many metals unified."

The discovery of metamorphosis in Italy in 1786-7 and his essay of 1790 on *Metamorphosis in Plants* form a continuum with the moral and spiritual concerns that extend both before and after these dates and indeed throughout his life. In talking about it Goethe even described the *Italian Journey* as a fairy tale. "The only kind of life which can be the concern of art is at once fully truthful and a pleasant story, a fairy tale."[30] Further, in whichever direction one follows, these imaginations, either in imagery or association, lead toward architecture.

Even in detail one could follow this through. The fan palm which Goethe sees in the botanical gardens in Padua and which marks an important stage in his discovery of metamorphosis, has reference to freemasonry and Greek mythology. It has an obvious architectural association in the similarity of the trunk of the palm to a column. Many of the freemasonry lodges in Continental Europe named themselves after palms.[31] As has been mentioned and as the name suggests, Masonry traces its origins to a building, that of Solomon's temple.

---

30. *Goethe's Briefe.* HA 3, 308. Quoted in Schultz, p9.
31. Curl, p144.

Amrine explores the rich associations in Goethe's imagination of the palm and follows them back to the sacred palm in Delos, "which Leto was said to have embraced in the pangs of giving birth to Apollo and Artemis."[32]

As in his encounter with the Mignon-like girl and the old harper,[33] his experience of the fan palm in Padua seems to be a meeting point between what works in Goethe's imagination and what he actually encounters on his Italian journey. The palm tree has deep symbolic meaning for Goethe as for other Freemasons, but the palm he sees in the Botanic Gardens is real enough and can still be seen today.

Goethe talks about the "open secrets" of nature. Here we touch upon one of his open secrets. The imagination is not something that passively records like a photograph or even something that draws upon our experience to produce a fanciful reality. Morally and spiritually, the artist works into the world in a creative way. This creativity does not stop at the world of thoughts and ideas. The architect creates buildings; the artist creates color and form. What then is the field of creation of the poet?

Goethe's interests in such fertile imaginations as these that have proved a rich source for many artists and writers did not preclude more conventional scientific research, nor his interest in encouraging this at Weimar and the nearby University of Jena. Goethe saw imagination as a polarity to sense-perception, but the scientist as much as the artist or poet needs both in order to be a fully-rounded human being.

His researches into the intermaxilliary bone and whether or not it existed in the human being were clearly undertaken with the eyes of the senses. Goethe's painstaking observations led him to overturn conventional scientific thinking of the day. Almost all the other scientists he knew were firmly of the opinion that there

---

32. Amrine, F. *Goethe's Italian Discoveries as a Natural Scientist.* p73. In: Hofmeister et al. *Goethe in Italy.*
33. IJ, September 7th.

was no intermaxilliary bone to be perceived in the human being. He visited and corresponded with some of the leading anatomists of the day who asserted this in the strongest terms. It was his imagination that gave Goethe the conviction that this bone would be found in the human being.[34] He felt that there must be physical continuity between the animal and the human. What differentiated them was that the human being had attained a higher moral and spiritual development, not a physical discontinuity.

In a similar vein are his studies in the field of geology. This interest developed when he was given ministerial responsibility for mines. He collected rock samples at all stages of his Italian journey and commented on the conflict between Neptunists and Vulcanists about the origins of the earth. His writings however, such as *On Granite*,[35] show an imaginative basis to the study. The same could be said of all his scientific writings: they rest upon both sense perception and imagination.

"Imagination" is not used here in the sense of "fanciful and unreal." Rather, it is used in the sense in which Goethe in the *Italian Journey* makes the distinction between "the eyes of the senses," and "the eyes of the spirit"; that is, between sense perception and that which represents a development of thinking to consider the "imponderable" things that we cannot see.

We can, and artists do, train themselves to look in a better way at things outside themselves. The perception of colors in a landscape by an artist who has learned to perceive them, for example, is more refined than the perceptions of people who have not developed that faculty in themselves. It is of course possible to use instruments to measure in an artificial way the variation in color. However there is the crucial difference that in the artist, it is developed by hard work and practice, by self discipline, and by

---

34. See the essay by Dorothea Kuhn, *Goethe's Relationship to the Theories of Development of his Time*, pp9-10, in *Goethe and the Sciences: A Reappraisal*, edited by Amrine, Wheeler and Zucker., Dordrecht: 1987.
35. Miller, D. *Goethe: Scientific Studies*, Volume 10 of the Suhrkamp Collected Works, New York: 1988, p131ff.

developing the moral strength to perceive these subtle variations. Whereas in the machine, although in certain respects the process may be more accurate, it is done in an artificially constructed way. Another analogy would be the wisdom a master craftsman has in his hands. Compare the skill of a master carpenter hammering nails accurately at great speed with the clumsy movements of an unpracticed amateur.

What distinguishes artists from machines, and equally master masons from craftsmen, is that artists like architects have developed their thinking qualitatively. It has become capable of perceiving the moral and spiritual and applying it to life as "invention" rather than "imitation." It has metamorphosed into imagination. Both "the eye of the senses" and "the eye of the spirit" are capable of qualitative development.

We can clarify what Goethe meant by the imagination from a different aspect. Douglas Miller in his introduction to *Goethe's Scientific Studies* speaks of Goethe's demand that the scientist "develop new organs of perception to participate in natural processes actively, objectively and imaginatively."[36] Goethe then gives the following example:

> When I closed my eyes and lowered my head, I could imagine a flower in the center of my visual sense. Its original form never stayed for a moment; it unfolded, and from within it new flowers continuously developed with colored petals or green leaves. These were no natural flower; they were fantasy flowers but as regular as rosettes carved by a sculptor...28
> Here the appearance of an after image, memory, creative imagination, concept, and idea all work simultaneously, revealing themselves through the unique vitality of the visual organ in complete freedom and without intention or direction.[37]

---

36. *Goethe: Scientific Studies*, pxix.

The difference I have been trying to make between 'the eye of the senses" and "the eye of the spirit" is implied in this passage. Goethe begins by saying, "I closed my eyes"; later, he refers to the activity he has described as revealing itself "through the unique vitality of the visual organ." Although what he describes in this passage has obvious similarities to a meditation exercise, it is not influenced primarily by any Eastern school such as Buddhism, but rather draws on Western traditions such as are found in Rosicrucian teachings and in freemasonry.

Let us now turn to two earlier works by Goethe in order to indicate something more that characterizes the working of Goethe's imagination: first, the fragment on *Nature* and then, from the side of art, the essay on Strasbourg Minster. Although the attribution of the prose poem, *Nature*, to Goethe is contested, Goethe clearly states that it expresses his attitude to nature in 1783 when it was published.[38] In this fragment nature is given a personality as "an unfathomable, limitless, humorous, self-contradictory being."[39] The fact that it was for some time regarded as written by Goethe suggests that there is much in it that other people found in tune with what Goethe writes elsewhere about nature, or, rather, *how* he writes about nature as a being.

Much of Goethe's imagination as it is expressed in his critical writings is conversational in nature. He was a great conversationalist[40] and this seems to have extended into how he thought things through in his imagination. The early essay on the architecture of Strasburg Minster is written in part as a conversation with the spirit of the builder which Goethe sees as still living in the design of the building.

---

37. Quoted in *Goethe: Scientific Studies*, pxix.
38. Goethe, *A Commentary on the Aphoristic Essay "Nature,"* in *Goethe: Scientific Studies*, pp6-7.
39. *Goethe: Scientific Studies*, p6.
40. Perhaps the easiest approach to Goethe and his work is through the *Conversations with Eckerman*, translated by J. Oxenford, London, 1930.

How often the gentle light of dusk, as it fused the countless parts into unified masses, soothed my eyes weary from intense searching. Now all stood before my soul, simple and great, and I full of bliss, felt develop in me the power at the same time to enjoy and understand. Then I sensed the genius of the great builder. "Why are you so amazed?" he whispered, "All these masses were necessary...[41]."

This essay is an autobiographical piece dedicated to the memory of the builder, Erwin von Steinbach. However Goethe does not just say, this or that happened to me. He tries to reveal what his inner experience was. He opens out the working of his imagination, often with a self-deprecating humour and a touch of irony. What happens inside and what happens outside are often presented as a kind of encounter. Out of the meeting a conversation occurs.

In Venice, Goethe refers to a similar conversation with Palladio.

When I meditated about how much justice or injustice I was doing to this extraordinary man, I felt as if he were standing beside me and saying: "That and that I did unwillingly, but did it nevertheless, because under the existing circumstances it was the only way that I could come very close to my most sublime idea."[42]

Goethe was someone who took great pleasure in conversation but in both these examples the conversation is in Goethe's imagination and with someone who is not physically present, except through works of architecture. In this last example, not only is the person of Palladio externalised, but the conversation is, as it were, outside of what Goethe knows. Goethe is wondering whether he is

---

41. Goethe, *On German Architecture,* in: *Goethe's essays on Art and Literature,* edited by J. Geary, translated by E. and E.H. von Nardroff, Volume 3 of the Suhrkamp Collected Works, New York: 1986, p6.
42. *IJ, October 6th,* p70.

right or wrong in his opinion about Palladio; then, Palladio appears beside him in his imagination and gives him another point of view, a thought previously unknown to Goethe. Although the conversation is internalised, it brings him another point of view from "outside." This seems to be a curious feature of imagination. In philosophical terms it is contradiction, a synthetic and an *a priori* way of knowing. Goethe however is as clear about his own inner life of thought and imagination as he is about his perceptions.

In his *Tale of the Green Snake and the Beautiful Lily* one of the riddles posed to the snake by the kings in the underground temple is, "What is more refreshing than Light?" The snake knows the answer: "Conversation."[43]

A final thought about how the essay on Strasbourg Minster shows the working of Goethe's imagination is that when he tries to describe the great idea that inspired Erwin von Steinbach's architecture, he puts it in terms that could be applied to a work of art or a work of nature:

> …it soars like a towering, widespreading tree of God. With its thousands of branches and millions of twigs and as many leaves as sands by the sea, it shall proclaim to the land the glory of the Lord, its master.

In this passage as elsewhere, Goethe's imagination seems to move easily between architecture and nature.

---

43. Goethe, *Conversation of the German Refugees,* Suhrkamp Collected Works, Vol. 10, p74.

Chapter 3

The Way to All Art and Life

Upon his arrival in Vicenza, Goethe exclaims, referring to Palladio: "There is really something Godlike about his designs."[1] He certainly seems to perceive in Palladio not just a great artist, but someone who embodies moral and spiritual greatness. As such, he becomes a guide for Goethe on his quest for what will cure him of his own moral and spiritual sickness—the illness which he writes about later in Venice.[2]

Goethe gives great weight to the effect of Palladio, although he does it in a self-deprecating and humorous way. He makes the comparison of the effect of Palladio to that of an illumination and compares it to Jacob Boehme's supreme moment of revelation while looking at a Pewter dish:

> The way to it [ancient times] and to all art and life has been opened for me by Palladio. This may sound a little odd, but surely not as paradoxical as Jacob Bohme's being enlightened about the universe after having received an influx of Jovian radiance from the sight of a pewter bowl![3]

---

1. *IJ, September19th,* p48.
2. *IJ, October 12th,* p82.
3. *IJ, October 8th,* p74.

In *Goethe and Alchemy* R.D. Grey[4] asserts that this is the only direct reference to Boehme in the whole of Goethe's writings. If true, this is surprising as Goethe's mother belonged to a pietist sect, which would certainly have knowledge of Boehme and his writings. The doctor who administered the powerful elixir when a serious illness brought the young Goethe to the point of death[5] belonged to this group. Is there some reference here to the fact that this earlier illness occurred when he was eighteen and a half and this more recent one when he was twice that age at thirty-seven? He had gained an alchemical understanding of life as process during his recovery from his first illness. He gained a deeper understanding of life and art from Palladio which helped to cure him of his second illness. Shortly after this reference he visits the Lido and, seeing some crabs there, exclaims, "What an exquisite, splendid thing a living creature is! How adapted to its condition, how genuine, how existent!"[6]

If he had learned anything of Palladio's biography, perhaps he was aware too that it was toward the end of his thirties when Palladio emerged from his anonymity, becoming a member of the Pedemure workshop in Vicenza with designs for his restoration—indeed his metamorphosis of—the Basilica in Vicenza. This followed Palladio's visit to Rome. Rome is Goethe's intended destination. He too is in his late thirties. On arriving there, he exclaims, "Although I am still the same person, I think I am changed to the very marrow of my bones."[7]

While I am speculating on what may have been the subtler associations in Goethe's imagination, it is part of this accumulation of coincidences that his illness when he was eighteen occasioned his move from Leipzig to Strasbourg, and thus was associated with his only other sizeable piece of writing that was specifically concerned with architecture prior to the sections in

---

4. Grey, p38.
5. Ibid., p5.
6. *IJ, October 9th*, p76.
7. *IJ, December 2nd*, p120.

the *Italian Journey* on Strasbourg Minster. Of course, it may be just coincidence that his two formative experience of architecture are so clearly associated with recovery from illness.

I have used the reference to Boehme as a springboard to leap through some of the various layers of meaning that have accrued to "Goethe" and which Goethe, the actual living eighteenth-century individual, seems to have almost playfully conspired in. An article by Gerhard Schulz clearly indicates the extent of the revisions Goethe made to the original journal and notes and the way he did it and comments that, "not even Goethe should have permitted himself these freedoms with Goethe manuscripts."[8]

Goethe speaks of Palladio's designs as having "the power of a great poet to take truth and lies and out of them frame a third entity, whose borrowed existence enchants us."[9] It seems to me that the Goethe one meets in the pages of the *Italian Journey* is just as much a construction as the buildings of Palladio, having a borrowed existence between "Poetry and Truth." The *Italian Journey* was indeed originally intended as a continuation of his autobiography.

The traveller Goethe is himself someone who has a borrowed existence. He travels under an incognito which he maintains even in Rome.[10] Furst points to the radical nature of Goethe's *Italian Journey*[11] with regard to the role that Goethe takes on within the narrative by introducing a doubling of himself: the one who is writing of the experiences and the one who is actually travelling and experiencing. She observes:

Whereas most travel literature draws its integration solely from the voice and personality of the narrating traveller, in

---

8. G. Schulz, *Goethe's Italienische Reise*, p5. In: Hoffmeister et al. *Goethe in Italy*, Amsterdam: 1988.
9. *IJ, September 19th*, p48.
10. *IJ, November3rd*, p106.
11. Furst, L. *Goethe's "Italienische Reise" in its European context*. In: Hofmeister, *Goethe in Italy*.

the case of the *Italienische Reise* there is in addition an artistic wholeness that devolves from its shaping by Goethe's creative imagination.[12]

Why did Goethe make all these changes? If he wanted a faithful account of the Italian journey why not just publish an edited version of the original journal and letters? Certainly such a version seems to read well enough. Dr. Reed even seems to have some preference for them over the published account. He suggests that they have more of an "authentic feeling" about them.[13]

His recovery from illness is certainly one of the themes of the account Goethe did publish of this part of the journey and, as we have noted, it is connected with his experience of Palladio's architecture. It led him to Vitruvius, thus providing him a way to approach the works of the ancient writers again.

On the surface,[14] this stands very strangely with one of the other themes we have mentioned: "Can the creases be eradicated that have formed and fixed themselves in my heart?" Here, far from wanting to engage with the classics, he seems to wish to free himself from the wrinkles of old habits: he is clearly searching for a new approach to looking at things. As Victor Lange has remarked he wanted "to test himself, his powers of perception, and his capacities for growth, to fathom his own intellectual and emotional resources."[15] Goethe's remark is made in the context of having to do things for himself again, as well as living in a locality that is new to him.

The pages that recount his arrival in Italy are full of observations about the way plants are cultivated there, how things grow in a different environment. This passage is echoed when he visits

---

12. Furst, L. p123. In: Hofmeister, *Goethe in Italy.*
13. T.J. Reed, *The Flight to Italy,* p 1X.
14. See Jantz, H., *Discovering Goethe,* p38. In: Bernd et al. *Goethe Proceedings at University of California, Davis.* South Carolina: 1984.
15. Lange, V. *Goethe's Journey in Italy: The School of Seeing,* p147. In: Hofmeister, *Goethe in Italy.*

the Botanical Garden in Padova: "We eventually think no more about plants we are accustomed to, like other long familiar objects; and what is observation without thought?"[16]

Again it is the newness and freshness that are opening his eyes.

When he is travelling from Verona to Vicenza he notices swags of grapes hanging down and adds, "Here one can form an idea of what festoons are!"[17] Similarly in Verona he speaks about Italian clock time which varies with the length of daylight and points out that they live closer to nature in Italy and do not "compare two clock hands together" to know what time of day it is.[18] The new experiences all seem to lead him outwards to nature. Art seems to lead him inwards and back to the past. Perhaps this dichotomy explains why in Venice he declares his intention to devote himself to science and handicrafts in future. "For the time of beauty is over, our day demands only what is an urgent and strict necessity."[19]

The polarity we have referred to earlier—between art and nature—here begins to emerge more clearly. We have indicated in Chapter 2 the polarity between seeing with the imagination and seeing with the senses. In speaking about Palladio's architecture, Goethe refers to the contradiction in combining columns and walls.[20] Here Goethe is pointing to another polarity, this time in architecture.

It seems to be a feature of the way Goethe looked at phenomena. Grey quotes an undated note from about the time of the Italian journey in which Goethe writes,

During the progressive transformation of the parts of a plant a power is active, which I call expansion or contraction, although the expression is really inadequate. It would be better to represent it, in algebraic fashion, by an x or a y,

---

16. *IJ, September 27th*, p54.
17. *IJ, September 19th*, p47.
18. *IJ, September 17th*, p43.
19. *Flight, October 5th*, p73.
20. IJ, September 19th, p48.

for the words expansion and contraction do not express the effect in its entirety.[21]

In connection with this, one can consider how in his *Commentary on the Aphoristic* essay "Nature" he says that one of the things he did not understand when the essay was written was *"polarity."*[22] In the *Metamorphosis of Plants,* written after the *Italian Journey,* Goethe points to such a progressive contraction and expansion in the plant's development. The seed expands into a leaf. The leaves at a certain point contract into the calyx, followed by an expansion into the petals of the flower, and so on through the pollen to the fruit where, in a final contraction, the new seeds are formed.

Looking at this section of the journey one begins to see how the polarity of art and nature informs the structure of it, especially if one substitutes architecture as one of the poles. There are of course comments on painting and sculpture, but the focus in this section is on architecture.

Our earlier question—why in rewriting this account did Goethe choose to emphasis this polarity between art and nature?—at first seemed to point in the direction of Goethe connecting himself with the classical world. However, Palladio was not a classical architect in the sense of someone who worked in the time of Ancient Greece or Rome. Relative to Goethe's lifetime, he was a fairly recent architect. He had struggled himself as to how to find a proper relationship to the past just as Goethe was trying to find a way to rewrite *Iphigenie.*

In Spoleto, Goethe speaks about the two great impressions he has received—from Palladio and Raphael. What impresses him, he says, is that "there wasn't a hair's breadth of arbitrariness in their work."[23]

---

21. Quoted in Grey, p61.
22. *Goethe: Scientific Studies,* p6.
23. *Flight,* p98.

Seeing the architecture of Palladio leads Goethe to understand the way to all art and life. Understanding the way "the primal force of nature" comes to expression also involves seeing a kind of architecture. It requires observation, not of the way the architect creates form in his buildings, but the creative process by which nature brings form into her creations.

In an essay, *Towards a General Comparative Theory*,[24] where he speaks of the way in which the "primal force of nature" is necessarily affected by the "diversity of height and depth, region and climate,"[25] he calls this "the mysterious architecture of the formative process."[26]

---

24. *Goethe: Scientific Studies*, pp53ff.
25. Ibid., p55.
26. Ibid.

CHAPTER 4

From the Brenner Pass to Venice

IN HIS WORK Goethe often makes analogies between architecture and nature. Even in a short piece such as that titled *An Unjust Demand*[1] he leaps from talking about the root of the plant to talking about "Strassburg and Cologne Cathedrals."

> ... our actual observation of the structure begins at the surface of the earth. The term ground plan is given to that part of the building which has reference to the floor, that part from which the structure then lifts itself upwards. The lower part, on which the higher or air-seeking part rests, is left to the skill, judgement and conscientiousness of the master builder. However, from the excellence and logic of the structure as a whole, we can easily draw conclusions as to the substructure.

> So, too, with the root. I was not concerned with it at all, for what had I to do with an organ which takes the form of strings, ropes, bulbs and knots, and – thus limited – manifests itself in such unsatisfying alternation, an organ where endless varieties make their appearance and where none

---

1. An unedited fragment found in Goethe's literary effects and published posthumously, dated June 27th, 1824, translated by Agnes Arber, in *Goethe's Botanical Writings*, p118.

advance. And it is advance solely that could attract me, hold me, and sweep me along on my course …"

In the *Italian Journey*, architecture is separated out, as it were, treated as a specific subject in its own right, and juxtaposed with other concerns rather than just being the stuff of analogy. This is not to suggest that at other times Goethe did not have an understanding of architecture; rather, that in the *Italian Journey* he wanted to treat it as a topic in its own right.

In the earliest entries there is very little mention of architecture except as asides: "In Bavaria one immediately comes upon the Waldsassen monastery." Yet even in such an innocuous remark he is already noting its site. "It lies in a basin, more like a dish than a kettle, in a lovely grassy hollow surrounded by gentle, fertile hills."[2]

At the very beginning though, the tone is set as a factual, almost scientific recording of the journey, illumined by the occasional statement of principle. "The smallest stream, once I have determined its direction of flow and the system it belongs to, quickly gives me a grasp of any region."[3]

Above Innsbruck he makes some observations about the weather. His interest is in how different kinds of clouds are formed and unformed.[4] He connects this with the "elasticity" of the air which in turn is connected with the "imperceptible" breathing of the earth. Though he himself makes fun of his fantastic speculation, he ties it to some exact sensory observations.

In the subsequent paragraphs he offers some observations about the plants he has seen around him.[5] However, he adds that his "hasty night-and-day trip was not conducive to any very fine observation"[6] and reflects that anyway, analysis "can

---

2. *IJ, September 3rd*, p14.
3. Ibid.
4. *IJ, September 8th*, pp19-20. Goethe's interest in the weather brought him into contact with the English scientist, Luke Howard. See Neenig, J. *Goethe and the English Speaking World*, Berne: 1988, pp192-3.
5. Ibid., pp20-21.
6. Ibid., p21.

never become my strong point. I direct my eyes at general characteristics".[7]

How is the same plant changed by growing on the plain or in the mountains? He answers: in the lower regions branches and stems are thicker and stronger, buds are closer together and leaves broader; whereas in higher regions branches and stems are more delicate, buds have greater intervals from node to node and leaves are more lanceolate.[8]

The general observations he gives here are developed in the *Metamorphosis of Plants* and his other botanical writings. Later writers such as Grohman have taken the observations Goethe makes about plants growing at different altitudes and in different localities and dealt with them more extensively.[9]

This section on plants is followed by more general observations about the rocks he has seen. At the end of this section Goethe mentions *Iphigenie* to which Herder has been telling him to give some attention. Goethe was not satisfied with the form he had given it.[10] Goethe did not just want to translate or imitate the original, but to rewrite it for his own age. He had brought the manuscript with him and symbolically, upon looking down into Italy, he takes it from his bag.[11] Again, one glimpses the structure in the *Italian Journey* which is drawn in so delicately. His problem with his play is related to that which he puts forth as a question about plants: How is the form of the plant affected by locality?

What *Iphigenie* was in Greek times cannot be the same as what the form of the story requires in Goethe's time. Goethe feels that he must change his physical environment, move to Italy and the

---

7. Ibid.
8. Although it belongs to a later section of the book, it is interesting to compare this with his description of the temples at Paestum.
9. The quotation at the end of Part 3 about the effect of the "diversity of height and depth, region and climate" on the "architecture of the formative process" is actually made with regard to their effect on animal form.
10. *IJ, September 8th*, p23.
11. Ibid.

beautiful, warm south where lemon trees grow, in order to have this form evoked.

To keep our theme clearly in sight let me transpose this process to Palladio who was also struggling with something that was taken from Greek times—the classical orders of architecture—and trying to find an appropriate form for them in his own time.

The next stage on Goethe's route is the detour to Lake Garda, which in Roman times was called "Benacus" and written of by Virgil: *"Fluctibus et fremitu resonans Benace marino."* One is reminded that in talking of his illness, he says that the sight of classical language had the power to make him ill.[12] This is the first line of classical verse that he has seen for himself: "…whose content has come to life before me…."[13] Here the past and the present form a continuity, unchanged: the line is tied in with the activity of nature.

Goethe has direct experience of its truth when he hires some men to row him down the lake in a small boat. They encounter a strong wind blowing in the opposite direction, which forces them to put in at Malcesine. From the boat Goethe catches sight of the old castle and goes out the next morning to sketch it, not realizing that it forms part of the Venetian line of defence against the Austrian empire. A crowd gathers around him, talking excitedly, and pointing to his drawing. Goethe thinks that they are admiring his drawing, so he is astonished when one of the men steps up to him, seizes the paper on which he is drawing and tears it in half. An altercation follows, during which the local official, the Podesta arrives.

The story which follows of how Goethe is almost arrested as a spy is told with Goethe's characteristic humour. For purposes of our study, what is interesting is a section that is presented as part of his argument with the crowd. The Podesta asks Goethe why he wants to draw a ruin which is of no artistic interest, unlike the ruins of classical buildings such as the Arena in Verona.

---

12. *IJ, October 12th*, p82.
13. *IJ, September 12th*, pp28-29.

In response, Goethe launches into an oration about the nature of the picturesque, which of course they don't understand, though Goethe seems to feel agreement on some "kindly female faces."[14]

The tale may have been embellished, but this is a discourse about the picturesque[15] right down to the ivy which "already had centuries of time to adorn the rock and masonry very richly."[16] It brings in not only the use of plants as adornments of buildings, but also the question of medieval versus classical buildings, and how we judge what is beautiful. With the lightest of touches, Goethe weaves this in with such questions as national differences, the common heritage of freedom, and the oppressiveness of large empires and petty tyrants (the Podesta and his assistant). Goethe puts his freedom, if not his life, on the line and asserts his rights as an artist in response to the Podesta's assertion that the only interesting thing about these walls is that the castle is a frontier fortress of the Venetian republic and is not to be spied upon. Goethe retorts: "I can boast as well as you to be the citizen of a republic."[17] Literally, he was born in the "free city" of Frankfurt; but perhaps, he refers to another kind of republic, that of artists.

This incident at Malcesine is a kind of polarity to later entries at Padova and Venice where botanical observations are made in the context of life in cities and the art and architecture they contain. Here at Malcesine though, the context for this debate about the aesthetic qualities of ruins is one where the emphasis is on the created works of nature: clouds and rivers, the lake and the mountains, the wind on the lake and the moon disappearing behind the mountain peaks. The social life too is that which is closely touched by nature. The freshness of the figs and the peaches, and the taste of the fresh trout from the lake are mentioned, along with the

---

14. *IJ, September 14th*, p31.
15. See Caroline van Eck, *Organicism in Nineteenth Century Architecture*, Amsterdam: 1994, pp82-3 where she considers the relationship between the Picturesque and Vitruvianism.
16. *IJ, September 14th*, p31.
17. Ibid., p32.

weather-beaten but handsome faces of the peasants who have no qualms about quenching their thirst from the puddles of water by the roadside from which their mules also drink.[18] Architecturally too, the castle at Malcesine is in contrast to the buildings of Palladio. It belongs to a different time, the medieval period.

The context changes when he comes to Verona, the first large Italian city he sees, and he begins to devote more space to architecture with a long passage on the old Roman amphitheater, the Arena: "the first significant monument of ancient times that I have seen, and so well preserved."[19] Two of the lines of thought he presents in this passage are: first, how such a form arises not quite naturally but humanly. Whenever there is a something to be seen, "people climb on benches, roll up barrels, drive up in carriages, pile up boards, occupy an adjacent hill, and quickly a crater is formed."[20] He then points out that the architect takes what is a "universal need" and meets it "by means of art."[21] He then adds: "the populace itself will be the decoration."[22]

There are also comments on the other buildings and public spaces, and generally the observations on art begin to replace the observations on nature. It is doubtless like the actual experience and so is true to life. However, we are reading in the *Italian Journey* something that was written almost thirty years after the event. Schultz states clearly that although the *Italian Journey* is based on the journals he kept and the letters he wrote when making the journey, it is in fact "an artistically constructed literary work, in which the form of a travel-diary is merely used as a narrative frame."[23] This suggests that this juxtaposition is constructed by Goethe.

---

18. Ibid., p34.
19. *IJ, September 16th*, p37.
20. Ibid.
21. Ibid.
22. Ibid.
23. Schultz, G. *Goethe's "Italienische Reise."* In: Hofmeister et al.*Goethe in Italy,* p6.

Equally, although there are comments about paintings, sculpture and drama, Goethe's comments become more and more focussed on the architecture he sees. A prominent aspect of this, from his arrival in Vicenza to the end of his stay in Venice, is Goethe's interest in the classical tradition of architecture traced back through Palladio to Vitruvius. Perhaps it reflected back to him some of his own concerns to find a suitable form into which he could recast *Iphigenie*.

Within a few hours of his arrival in Vicenza, Goethe had walked about the town and seen the "Olympian theatre and the buildings of Palladio."[24] On subsequent days he revisits the Olympian theatre to see an opera and again to hear a debate of the Academy of the Olympian on the theme: "whether invention or initiation has been of greater benefit to the fine arts."[25] He pays a visit to the old architect Scanozzi on Sept 21. Scanozzi had edited a four-volume work on Palladio's buildings. The same day Goethe visits the Rotonda, one of Palladio's most celebrated buildings. He notes how it has made use of the form of classical temples: "Each individual side would make a suitable view of a temple."[26] He notes then how Palladio's work is a metamorphosis of classical architecture. His first impression is that "there has never been more extravagant architecture." This is in strong contrast to what he will say later of Palladio, that there isn't "a hair's breadth of arbitrariness"[27] in his work. The journey his imagination takes is that metamorphosis is also a physical journey which gives him a deeper understanding of Palladio.

We can perhaps glimpse this in one of the sentences included in the opening entry on Vicenza that is not included in the relevant section in *Flight to Italy*. That is: "If you don't see these works on the spot you can have no real conception of them."[28] In the *Italian*

---

24. *IJ*, September 19th, p47.
25. *IJ*, September 22nd, p51.
26. *IJ*, September 21st, p50.
27. *Flight*, October 19th, p98.
28. *Flight*, September 19th, p43.

Journey he adds: "Only when these works are actually seen can one recognize their great merit; for they must fill the eye with their true size and concreteness and satisfy the spirit with the beautiful harmony of their dimensions, not only in abstract outlines but with all their projecting and receding parts seen in perspective."

By the time he reaches Venice he has acquired the works of Palladio and read them. He hurries into the "Carita" which he asserts to be "admirably designed both as a whole and in its individual parts."[29] Unfortunately, the whole plan was not carried through: "Scarcely a tenth part has been built though even this is worthy of his genius, having a perfection of arrangement and an exactness of execution that are beyond anything known to me. Years should be spent in contemplating such a work. I think that I have never seen anything more sublime or perfect, and I believe I am not mistaken. Let us imagine this excellent artist, born with an inner sense of the grand and gracious, who first, with incredible effort, attains to the cultural level of the ancients, so that he may re-establish them by himself."

The related part in the original documents (published as *Flight to Italy*) is dated October 11th not October 2nd. There is a shorter entry on the 2nd about the Carita, but much of this later entry has also been included in the entry in the *Italian Journey* for October 2nd. The following is part of the entry in *Flight to Italy* for October 11th: "The outstanding artist with an innate feeling for what is great, which he worked hard to cultivate (for people have no idea how much trouble he took over the works of Antiquity) finds an opportunity to carry out a favorite idea, to emulate a dwelling of the ancients, for once the idea exactly fits. There's nothing to get in his way, nor would he let anything."

(The Appendix includes in sequence many of the passages where Goethe speaks of architecture in general and in particular of Palladio. I also include part of the two "Nature" interludes: his visit to the Botanical Gardens in Padua and his visit to the seashore

---

29. *IJ*, October 2nd, p61.

at the Lido in Venice. What follows assumes a familiarity with those sections.)[30]

Goethe's imaginative process as presented in the *Italian Journey*, whether what really happened or a poetic construction by Goethe in his sixties, reaches a culmination during his two-week stay in Venice where, besides his entertaining comments on Venetian society, much emphasis is given to the architecture and particularly to how it stands in a humanly-constructed relationship to the water of the Lagoon. This being Goethe, it is often indicated with a light, witty touch. On the opening page of the Venice section, the city is introduced as "the beaver republic."[31] Later he compares the basilica of San Marco to an oversized crustacean.[32]

It is as though the predominant element of water effects a metamorphosis on the form of the buildings, much as in the earlier section when he refers to how the same plant growing low down on marshy ground or high up on mountain slopes will adapt itself accordingly.

Appendix I also includes relevant quotations about the architecture of Palladio in Venice. It will be apparent from those quotations as well as from a general reading of this part of the *Italian Journey* the extent to which Goethe is conscious of and stimulated by the watery element and fascinated by the relationship of the architecture to it.

Just as the Malcesine incident breaks into Goethe's musings about nature in the mountains and on the shores of Garda, so the architectural considerations in the Venice section are interrupted by a visit to the Lido where Goethe sees the sea for the first time in his life. By saying little about its effect on his imagination, he says much. Apart from wishing the children of his friends could be with him, he mentions a visit to the grave of Consul Smith who

---

30. See Appendix I starting on p61.
31. *IJ*, September. p56.
32. *Flight*, p62.

was involved in the publishing of the edition of Palladio he has acquired.[33]

He also records some observations he makes of plants growing on the shore and what effect the salty air has on them:

> …they are brimming with juices like water plants, they are firm and tough like mountain plants; in cases where the ends of the leaves have a tendency to become prickly, like thistles, these prickles are extremely pointed and strong.[34]

Earlier in Padua there is a similar interjection of nature when he visits the Botanical Gardens there. Here, schematically, is the structure I am suggesting for this section of the *Italian Journey*:

NATURE	TOWN & CITY (ARCHITECTURE)
Mountains and Lake Garda	*Malcesine*
	Verona
	Vicenza
Botanical Gardens	*Padua*
Lido / Sea Shore	*Venice*

Nowhere in these pages does Goethe offer a theory of architecture. Rather he draws in and accumulates a pattern of incidents which in their reading seem like markers of the path his imagination has travelled and which allows the reader to follow him. I will now consider in detail one of the journal entries, that for "Padua, September 28th," to show how this structure is carried down even into the parts.

In Padua after a visit to the anatomy theatre[35] where bodies are dissected, Goethe is refreshed by a visit to the Botanical

---

33. *IJ, October 8th*, p75.
34. Ibid., p76.
35. Goethe's own scientific interests moved from anatomical studies to plant studies which parallels what he does here. It may be coincidental or it may give an indication of the subtlety and wit with which Goethe's imagination works.

Gardens.[36] The two visits to the Botanical Gardens in *Flight to Italy*, on September 26th and 27th,[37] are compressed into one on September 27[th38] in the *Italian Journey*.

Whereas in *Flight to Italy* the visits are mentioned almost as an aside, in the *Italian Journey* much more significance is given. Quite a long section is added to what is recorded in the diary. First, the thought that we are stimulated by things with which we are not familiar. Then, that:

…in this newly encountered diversity that idea of mine keeps gaining strength, namely, that perhaps all plant forms can be derived from one plant. Only in this way would it be possible truly to determine genera and species, which, it seems to me, has hitherto been done very arbitrarily.[39]

In his *History of My Botanical Studies*, he emphasizes what a key moment this was for him in his discovery of metamorphosis, perhaps second only to his first actual experience of the plant archetype in the botanical gardens in Palermo.[40]

A few paragraphs on in the same entry for September 27th Goethe speaks of the works of Mantegna:

And now the liveliness of their genius, the energy of their nature, illuminated by the spirit of these predecessors and invigorated by their strength, could climb higher and ever higher, rise from the earth and bring forth heavenly but true

---

36. Taverner, R. *Palladio and Palladianism*, London: 1991, p46. These gardens were designed by Daniel Barbaro, whose family were Palladio's patrons at Maser and in Venice and for whom Palladio made drawings for his edition of *Vitruvius*.
37. *Flight*, p55.
38. *IJ*, pp53-4.
39. Ibid., p54.
40. Amrine, F. *Goethe's Italian Discoveries as a Natural Scientist (The Scientist in the Underworld)*, p62. In: Hoffmeister et al. *Goethe in Italy*. He refers to Agnes Arber, a famous Goethean botanist, who argued that the whole of Goethe's work on the *Metamorphosis of Plants* could be viewed as "the reasoned outcome of the meditation that began to take shape beside the palm tree at Padua."

forms. It was thus that art developed after the barbarous times.[41]

In this "rise higher from the earth," "climb higher and higher," and "bring forth heavenly but true forms," such expressions mirror the images he uses to talk about the plant, though here he is talking about the development of art. In his commentary on the essay *Nature*, Goethe writes about "the two great driving forces" he did not perceive when that essay was written. They are:

> ... *polarity* and *intensification,* the former is a property of matter insofar as we think of it as material, the latter insofar as we think of it as spiritual. Polarity is a state of constant attraction and repulsion, while intensification is a state of ever striving ascent.[42]

Polarity we have considered. Intensification would seem to be what he is talking about when he speaks about how Mantegna in his paintings developed what he had received as illumination from the spirit of his predecessors. Here, though, he is talking about the development of art, not the "great driving forces" of nature.

Immediately afterwards he gives a brilliant short description of one of the most striking architectural features in Padova, the Salone. Unlike the section on Mantegna, this description is not in *Flight to Italy.* He says that it "produces a curious sensation" and then gives a very striking description. He says it is more like the feeling of being drawn out of ourselves than the feeling of being gently pressed back into ourselves. He points here to one of life's archetypal experiences of polarity, the polarity of in-breathing and out-breathing, that of sleeping and waking, and he even brings in the feeling of being enclosed within something in contrast to the feeling of being open to the starry sky. This polarity draws from an architectural experience. It clearly relates to the

---

41. *IJ*, p55.
42. *Goethe: Scientific Studies*, p6.

fundamental polarity he points to in the development of a plant, that between expansion and contraction.

The realization of this as something that works in every part of all plants, but in the leaf particularly, as the way in which form is created, was part of the experience for Goethe of the fan palm in the Botanical Gardens[43] which now is called, *Palma di Goethe*. In his introduction to Goethe's botanical writings, Charles Engard says:

> Of all the plants in the garden, the one which influenced him most was the fan palm, for he noted, its leaves exhibited a complete series of transition forms from the simple lance-shaped first leaves to the most complex fan type. This observation seems to have been the nucleus from which the doctrine of metamorphosis was to grow.[44]

This is confirmed by Goethe in his plant studies where he records how he had the gardener cut off "an entire sequence of modifications" for him which he still had at the end of his life in 1831 and which was still capable of "attracting and engaging my attention completely."

It is strange then that he never mentions this plant in the *Italian Journey* or in *Flight to Italy*.[45] However, much of this entry for September 27th draws out themes that belong to the experience of nature for him: the sequence of intensification in a plant's development and the polarity which provides the alternating stages of this sequence. Both of these are fundamental perceptions for understanding metamorphosis.

This section does not talk about what Goethe experienced of the fan palm or of other plants in the botanical garden directly,

---

43. *IJ*, p55.
44. Mueller, B. (trans). *Goethe's Botanical Writings*, p6.
45. Curl, J.S. *Art and Architecture of Freemasonry*, p144. Curl points out that "the palm tree had powerful Masonic connections in continental Europe." Many lodges were named after different types of palms.

but reveals this through his experience of painting and architecture. Goethe was here drawing upon what he had experienced in the fan palm but presenting it through his experience of art, suggesting that in his imagination where he structured the *Italian Journey,* the two types of experience were interchangeable and perhaps even identical.

This whole entry seems to be a meditation on the relationship between nature and art. Through his characterization of Mantegna's role in art he writes of "intensification" and in the description of the Salone he refers to a fundamental "polarity" of life. Appropriately, in the penultimate paragraph, he depicts himself meditating in a church, a vast but simple building. No one "would have looked for me there."[46]

The whole entry commences with the words, "At last I have acquired the works of Palladio…"[47] This position gives it more emphasis than it has in *Flight to Italy* where it does not start the entry and is introduced by the words, "Another thing I did today…"[48]

The *Italian Journey* then elaborates a conversation in the bookstore where he buys the *Quattro Libri* with some other gentlemen about the relative merits of Palladio and Vitruvius. This, of course, introduces the theme that is later worked on in what Goethe writes about Mantegna in relationship to ancient art. Whether or not the conversation in the bookstore actually did occur and whether its content was as Goethe reports it is perhaps of less importance than clearly understanding the theme that Goethe is introducing here in connection with buying a copy of Palladio's major written work. This will lead in Venice to him buying a copy of Vitruvius. As if to emphasis the point, this is recorded in the same place toward the end of the Venice section where he makes a confession about his secret malaise which

---

46. *IJ*, p55.
47. *IJ*, p52.
48. *Flight*, p57.

necessitated his journey to Italy. He continues, "Palladio through his words and works, his manner of thought and action, has already brought Vitruvius closer to me and interpreted him better than the Italian translation can do."[49]

One of the symptoms of his illness was that he could not look at a page of classical writing without becoming ill. By the time he reaches Venice something has cured him of that.

He has learnt also to look at things in a new way. He can write:

> The revolution that I foresaw and that is now going on within me is the same as has happened to every artist who for a long time was diligently true to nature and now beheld the remains of the great ancient spirit, his soul swelled within him and he felt a kind of inward transfiguration of himself, a feeling of freer life, higher existence, lightness and grace.[50]

One feels a relatedness of this passage to what he writes in Padua about Manegna. However in Venice he seems to be talking not about historical and cultural processes, but rather about a personal metamorphosis. This metamorphosis works off a polarity between his sense experiences of nature and art on the one hand, and on the other, the way his imagination has been enlivened by the same experiences. This polarity has been intensified through his personal feelings. Both the historical and cultural process and the individual process seem like different reflections of the process he has uncovered in the development of the plant. He has been led to this by coming to understand how Palladio works in architecture. At least we may suggest that it was when he was looking at the architecture of Palladio that he deepened his understanding of what the process of metamorphosis was.

---

49. *IJ,* p82.
50. *Flight,* p64.

CHAPTER 5

The School of Seeing

EARLY IN THE JOURNEY Goethe sets himself the task of developing his powers of seeing. Reading the *Italian Journey* you become aware of how seriously Goethe took this resolve. You also become aware of what he was trying to achieve. Not only are the insights he gained into the creative life of nature and the nature of architecture interesting in themselves, but as you follow the sequence of observations and experiences he records you are caught up in a process which shows the way "to all art and life."

As we have pointed out though, his interest in Palladio was much more to do with how Palladio had taken the classical approach to architecture and used it to develop what was in his own imagination: the great idea he carried in his mind.

The question was not: how do we get back to classical times? Rather it was: how do we bring what was there in the past into the present and metamorphose it into a form appropriate for our time? How does metamorphosis work with regard to different periods of art? Although nothing emerges as a theory of architecture, Goethe did take in hand the other part of the search—how nature works in creating form—and wrote his essay on the *Metamorphosis of Plants* after returning from Italy. Clearly this derived from his experiences in Italy. Essays in *Goethe and the Sciences: A Reappraisal* make frequent reference to them.[1]

---

1. Brady, R.H. *Goethe's Morphology,* pp267ff; Portman, A. *Goethe and the Concept of Metamorphosis,* pp133ff. In Amrine et al. (eds) *Goethe and the Sciences: A Reappraisal.*

In section 20 of the essay on *The Metamorphosis of Plants*,[2] he refers to "the date palm" which "affords a striking example of such graded diversification of the simplest leaf form." In *History of My Botanical Studies,* he is more specific.

I experienced the fullness of this foreign vegetation most strongly; however, when I entered the Botanical Gardens at Padua ... A date palm captured my full attention; fortunately, the simple, lanceolate primary leaves still stood on the ground; the successive articulation of the leaves increased until the mature fan stood revealed. Finally, there emerged from within a spathe-like husk a twig with blossoms and appeared to be a development that bore no relationship to the previous growth, alien and astonishing. ...[3]

Although Goethe had written short accounts of his botanical discoveries, he still found it worthwhile to work on the *Italian Journey*, which provided the autobiographical and artistic aspects connected with this discovery, and this gave a fuller picture of it.

Insofar as *The Metamorphosis of Plants* is concerned, to record not so much what he saw, but how he saw things, suggests that one of the themes he wanted to present in the *Italian Journey* was the development of this way of seeing.

Here one moves into strange ground for the twenty-first-century reader. It would not occur to most people to consider the *how* of seeing.

This is usually taken to be a physiological given: you cannot learn how to see better. If such a thought does occur in present-day conversation, it tends to be in the context of genetics or a visit to the opticians rather than education.

---

2. *Goethe: Scientific Studies*, pp76-80.
3. Translated in: Amrine, F. *Goethe's Italian Discoveries as a Natural Scientist*, p61. In Hofmeister et al. *Goethe in Italy*.

In the eighteenth century the moral aspect of how you looked at things was seen as important. Sir Joshua Reynolds' lectures on art at the Royal Academy in London are concerned with the training of the artist. This in turn is concerned with how the artist looks at things as a form of better seeing and moral improvement. This tone is still found in Ruskin. The artist's road was one of moral improvement and this higher morality, the imagination, the schooled seeing of the artist, could then be used more widely to improve public morals.[4] This was especially the case with the architect whose work so directly affected the public who had his work all around them.

In Malcesine we see Goethe as educator of "the birds," explaining to them how to look at the old castle. How could they be expected to recognize the beauty of something with which they were so familiar?

As he addresses them, the morning sun illuminates the view with a lovely light which makes the old castle look even more beautiful. Goethe is pointing to something undeniable: the effect of light on a building. Although it is not quite a matter of life and death with him, in the narrative he does connect the aesthetic act, the seeing of beauty in things, with whether or not he will be arrested, that is, with his state of freedom. This may be just as it happened, but the effect of light on buildings is very important and not only for their picturesque appeal. Many of Palladio's buildings are built in relation to the light. Peter Murray, writing about The Redentore points out: "The play of light changes constantly in the simple pale interior so that there is an almost endless succession of spatial effects, varying according to the time of day and the season of the year."[5]

In Palladio and Vitruvius, the relationship of a building to the light is seen as both practical and moral, as both healthy and

---

4. Goethe's position is clearly presented in his essay on *Winckelmann and his Age*, p99ff in Volume 3 of the Suhrkamp collected edition.
5. Murray, P. *Architecture of the Italian Renaissance*, London: 1969. p223.

beautiful.[6] It is obviously advantageous to have certain rooms facing south to catch the light and other cooler rooms on the north side. However, the architect must be educated to understand the moral effect of his work. Good architecture brings about a good people, both by working aesthetically through their senses and by working morally through their imagination. This is the tradition to which Reynolds and Ruskin gave expression and which stretches back through Palladio and Vitruvius. It is the classical tradition which Goethe was encountering when he looked at a page of classical text.

Goethe was aware of this tradition. He had even written a "classical" play, *Iphiginie in Tauris*. He took this as a precious burden with him to Italy and takes it out of his bag at the same time as he comes to the place where he sees with his own eyes something that is mentioned in a line of Virgil—where the "dead letter" comes alive. There is in this juxtaposition perhaps another delicate suggestion of what the moral problem was which caused his "malaise."

When Goethe speaks of the "malaise" which affected him before leaving for Italy and gives it as the reason for his abrupt departure, he does not talk about his symptoms as headaches or other aches. Rather, he says that when he looked at a page of Latin writing he was so affected that he could not do anything for days afterward. This is the secret of his "malaise." He is a writer and he speaks thus of looking at a page of classical text. This is a moral and an artistic effect that strikes down into the physical—in the terms we use in Chapter 2 it is to do with the "imagination" rather than sense-perception. In our time we would probably call it "writer's block." There can be no physiological reason why a page of Latin text makes him ill. He explains it further and speaks of his great longing for the land where the words were written.

It is the dead letter which incapacitates him in contrast to the life which has given form to these sounds. In the plant we can

---

6. Examples are in: Palladio. *Second Book*, Chapters XIII and XVI; Vitruvius, BOOK VI, Chapter VII, paragraphs 6 and 7.

look at the "dead letter" of its form or we can look for the life which has taken on the form. In architecture we can look abstractly and theoretically at the forms or we can consider them as an expression of the imagination of the architect. It all depends upon how we look at them.

It was against Goethe's nature to make theories about things. In such abstract thinking a series of phenomena is taken and the finished material result given an empty name which has no reference or connection to the process by which the phenomena came into being. He writes of Venice as, "a hollow name that has often made me uneasy, me, the mortal enemy of verbal sounds."[7]

The facts of nature can similarly be approached through an abstract, intellectual, classifying process and then given a "hollow name." Goethe was more concerned about researching the phenomena and out of them to try to follow a half-hidden track to the archetype of the phenomena. What is the life process that comes to expression in the phenomena of nature? What is the imagination that comes to expression in a work of architecture?

In abstract thinking one takes a series of phenomena, then examines the finished material result and not the process by which the phenomena came into being. It is this last process, by which the form is created, that interested Goethe because he felt that not only did it explain what all plants had in common, but it also was the selfsame process which the imagination followed in creating a work of art.

"How Palladio worked" became increasingly clear to Goethe. This "how" was the process of Palladio's imagination. In understanding it, Goethe understood "the way to all art and life"; for what both processes have in common—that of nature and that of the imagination—is metamorphosis. He identified "intensification" and "polarity" as the essential qualities of the process of becoming. These principles carried over to architecture and, to Goethe's seeing, are what one might call the alchemy of architecture.

---

7. *IJ, September, 28th*, p56.

Chemistry analyzes substance, and the alchemy of substance which preceded it tried to understand the transformation of matter through heating, dissolving and so on. Architecture works on the transformation of space.[8] What is space to start off with but a seeming nothingness: the polarity of substance and the antithesis of form. Working on space is like working on the negative image. Similarly, the form of the leaf is elaborated out of the unformed substance of the cotyledons.

Some will quarrel that the space is nothing in itself. What architecture does is create fine façades and exemplary interiors, but surely there is more. When you walk into Il Redentore, even before you notice what is around you, you notice the space; you sense the space which is unlike any you have experienced before.

Outside, too, a building can define a space. What would the view of Venice be like without San Giorgio or Vicenza without the Basilica and the Loggia? The Piazza dei Signori is clearly a created, a formed, space, though an external space open to the sky.

Let us try and approach this from a different direction. If we look at the variety of plant forms, even restricting ourselves to the annual plants, we see such a huge variety that it is sometimes difficult to see what they all have in common that we can call them plants.[9] One could say exactly the same thing about buildings, even restricting them to those belonging to the Western Classical tradition. Considering only their external form, we likewise see a great variety. Yet we intuitively feel there is a connection between the Pantheon in Rome and the Villa Caprese (Rotonda) near Vicenza. We can to some extent reconstruct the thoughts which passed through the minds of the builders of both these buildings.

---

8. Palladio, *Quattro Libri*, p351, note 90. In this note, mention is made of the difficulty of translating "Aere, che sara tra I vani." Literally it means, "the air that will be between the spaces" (of the columns). The translators, Taverer and Schofield, comment that "it does not make sense in English."
9. This is the question that stimulates Goethe to the imagination of the plant archetype in Sicily. *IJ, April 17th*, p214. It echoes his thoughts in Padua, *September 27th*, p54, "perhaps all plant forms can be derived from one plant."

Writing about the villas of Palladio, Wittkower asserts, "While in looking at these façades nobody can escape the impression that an inexhaustible wealth of ideas has gone into them, one should not lose sight of the fact that they are all generated from the same basic pattern."[10] However, we do not know of any similar thinking process that is connected with the creation of diverse forms in the plant kingdom.

Is Goethe's question, "How do I know this or that thing is a plant," any more strange than the question, "How do I know this or that thing is a building?"

If we give Goethe's question due consideration, it is evident that it is not intended in a superficial sense, but it is related to the "bewildering variety of form" which we refer to as plants; that it is not asking what all these have in common, but what thoughts order the creation of their form.

Perhaps "thoughts" is an inappropriate word. It might be more suitable to use the word, "imaginations." In the formative meeting between Goethe and Schiller,[11] when Goethe had sketched out the plant archetype for him, Schiller insisted that what he had produced was "not an observation from experience" but "an idea." To which Goethe retorted, "Then I may rejoice that I have ideas without knowing it, and even see them with my own eyes."[12] In describing the plant archetype later, Goethe used the term, "an exact sensory imagination."[13] He says that although a scientist might find it hard to accept that such a thing exists, "art is unthinkable without it." By definition you would have to "see" such a thing. When he writes in the *Italian Journey*, "How (Palla-

---

10. Wittkower, R. *Architectura Principles of the Age of Humanism*, London: 1988, p73.
11. Goethe, *Fortunate Encounter*, pp18-21. In *Goethe: Scientific Studies*, Edited and translated by D. Miller.
12. Ibid., p20.
13. *Goethe: Scientific Studies*, p46. The use of the expression occurs in a review of Ernst Stiedenroth, *A Psychology in Clarification of Phenomena from the Soul*.

dio) thought and worked becomes increasingly clear to me,"[14] he is in the process of forming such exact sensory imaginations.

The purpose of this "Goethe" who discovers the metamorphosis sequence in nature through understanding the connection between art and nature is stated clearly: he asks, "Is my eye clear, pure, and bright, how much can I grasp in passing, can the creases be eradicated that have formed and fixed themselves on my heart?"[15] His task as stated here is to develop the how of seeing. But this "how" is not through the acquiring of moral traditions. Rather "I am only concerned with sense expressions ... trying my powers of observation, and testing the effect of my knowledge and scientific training."[16]

He does not reject the traditions, but feels they are unsuitable for his times. This is, after all, only a few years before the outbreak of the French Revolution.[17] He rather finds a kinship with Palladio who knowing "the petty narrowness of his own times" did his best as circumstances allowed, "not surrendering but determined to remodel everything in accord with his noble ideas."[18]

This is a different approach on the face of it to that of following the high tradition of art through Michelangelo and Raphael back to the classical period, which was announced by Reynolds at his Royal Academy lectures during the same period preceding the French Revolution. It is more akin to the approach of the experimental scientist. We just look at what is there. Looking in this way—going to nature—is the best educator of our senses. However, what one encounters there is not well-ordered and content, but wild and chaotic. It is the "nature" of the aphoristic essay.[19]

14. *IJ, October 6th*, p70.
15. *IJ, September 11th*, pp25-6.
16. Ibid., p25.
17. Padovan, R. *Proportion*, London: 1999, p10. Padovan argues for architectural proportions to be re-founded no longer on the basis of the "unity of nature and art" but on their "duality."
18. *IJ, October 3rd*, p63.
19. *Goethe: Scientific Studies*, pp3-5.

The problem was how to find a bridge between the two. There was on the one hand, a world of morality and order, the great classical artistic tradition, and on the other there was a world of often destructive chaos, the natural world. One of Goethe's first remembered events was the Lisbon earthquake. How was the human being related to nature on one hand and to art on the other? The study of nature increasingly excluded the role of imagination. The classical tradition had become a "dead letter." Both would lead to an unhealthy way of looking at things.

It is my suggestion in this essay that Goethe wrote the *Italian Journey* in part to show how he had discovered the bridge between how we look at art and how we look at nature. He does so by a structural juxtaposition in the book of nature and art, in particular architecture. Through this juxtaposition he points to how we can school our seeing to develop a higher form of seeing, imagination, which allows us to perceive the process of metamorphosis. This allows a "conversation" with the phenomena to begin.

This Goethean approach to the world, his way of looking at things, often finds clearest expression in his approach to the phenomena of nature. Of the arts perhaps it finds clearest expression in his sporadic writings on architecture. This may be partly because the form of buildings is most clearly allied to how we look at them.

To see a building is to engage directly with the creative process of the architect. Perhaps "to see" is the wrong expression, for there are certainly the solid parts of the building which one sees. But what of the spaces in the building; do we see them?

This brings us to Goethe's one "theoretical" piece of writing on architecture mentioned earlier.[20] Throughout the whole of this short essay one catches echoes of what he has to say about Palladio in the *Italian Journey*. For example, in one paragraph he speaks of the role of imitation and invention in architecture. This is exactly the question—though with reference to the arts in

---

20. Goethe, *Palladio, Architecture (1795)*. In Gage, J. *Goethe on Art.*

general—that Goethe heard debated at a meeting of the Olympian Academy when he was in Vicenza. There, though, in keeping with Goethe's general tone in the *Italian Journey*, it is treated much more lightly and with good humor. He noted how the audience generally applauded the arguments in favor of imitation but missed many of the good arguments made in favor of invention. Immediately preceding this is a long paragraph which is very revealing about his approach to architecture, about how he "saw" things.

It might very well be thought that, as a fine art, architecture works for the eye alone, but it ought primarily—and very little attention is paid to this—to work for the sense of movement in the human body. When, in dancing, we move according to certain rules, we feel a pleasant sensation, and we ought to be able to arouse similar sensations in a person whom we lead blindfold through a well-built house. The difficult and complicated doctrine of proportion, which enables the building and its various parts to have character, comes into play here.'[21]

---

21. Goethe, *Palladio, Architecture (1795)* pp196-7. In Gage, J. *Goethe on Art.*

Chapter 6

Conclusion

I HAVE TRIED to establish a general connection between Goethe's discovery of metamorphosis and his experience of Palladio's architecture. Given that, are there ways that one can point to a direct influence of Palladio on what eventually found expression in the *Metamorphosis of Plants*? There are indeed several, but they require us to go into a more detailed consideration of Goethe's botanical ideas. One of the most interesting aspects a study of Goethe's response to architecture reveals is the relationship between scientific and artistic study.

Perhaps the indications I have given of what Goethe saw in Palladio and how they gave him insight into his general idea of metamorphosis are sufficient. I have tried to follow the correspondence between Goethe's observations on the effect of locality on how a plant grows and what he writes about buildings being affected by their locality, such as in his comments about Venice. It is an interesting feature of Palladio's villas that he often "created" a landscape for them.[1]

The second parallel could be drawn by considering Palladio's variety of buildings. There are villas, town houses, palaces, churches, basilicas, and theatres, just as you have different kinds of plants. Palladio's creative activity stems from the great idea he had in his mind. The buildings fall short of this, but Palladio

---

1. Holberton, P. *Palladio's Villas*, p122ff.

always came as close to his idea as was possible in the circumstances. Compare this to how Goethe speaks of the plant archetype: "Here in this newly encountered diversity—that idea of mine keeps gaining strength, namely, that all plant forms can be derived from one plant."[2] The question that arises in both cases from this diversity is: Is there something from which it all derives?

In following this idea back through Palladio and Vitruvius, Goethe was going back in time to see how buildings were perceived in classical times and what it was Palladio had brought into our time from the classical age.

In Palladio's written works architecture is studied in its parts. The way the parts relate to the whole, to the "great idea" Palladio has in his mind, can be applied to create temples or basilicas and other buildings. One of the principles of classical architecture as interpreted by Palladio was that the whole can be seen in every part. This even extended to his providing reconstructions of buildings that were extant only as a ground plan.[3]

The way in which Goethe speaks of Palladio's "great idea" suggests he had some insight into it.

If so, then it could be that his statement that Palladio has shown him the way to all art and life means that he has understood how Palladio's idea of what architecture is lives in all his buildings. So too with the plant archetype which lives in all plants. Palladio has shown him the way to art, to architecture, and to life—to the plant archetype.

In Rome he could write that when you see the whole, of which you have hitherto only seen the parts, "then a new life begins."[4]

This is only scratching the surface of the question, for as has been evident throughout, this is only part of the whole journey. Indeed, writers such as Pevsner have seen much more importance

---

2. *IJ, September 27th*, p54.
3. Palladio, *Quattro Libri*, Book 4, Chapter XV. Speaking about the Temple of Mars, Palladio says, "I have endeavoured to represent it whole, by means of what I could collect from its ruins and from the doctrine of Vitruvius..."
4. *IJ, November1st*, p103.

in Goethe's comments about architecture as he journeyed further south.

Indeed, it goes without saying that the full picture of the "great idea" that Goethe carried in his mind (or should one say "imagination") only emerges in looking at the whole.

Appendix I

Quotations from Goethe's Italian Journey

⁓ *Italian Journey*, Vicenza, 19 September

I arrived here a few hours ago, have already walked about the town and seen the Olympian theatre and the buildings of Palladio. A very pretty little book with engravings and an expert text has been published for the convenience of foreigners. Only when these works are actually seen can one recognize their great merit; for they must fill the eye with their true size and concreteness and satisfy the spirit with the beautiful harmony of their dimensions, not only in abstract outlines but with all their projecting and receding parts seen in perspective. And so I say of Palladio: he was intrinsically and through and through a great man. The greatest difficulty confronting him, like all modern architects, was the proper use of the columnar orders in civil architecture; for to combine columns and walls is, after all, a contradiction. But how he has managed that! How he impresses with the presence of his works and makes us forget that he is only being persuasive. There is really something godlike about his designs, like the power of a great poet to take truth and lies and out of them frame a third entity, whose borrowed existence enchants us.

The Olympian theatre is a theatre of the ancients on a small scale and inexpressibly beautiful, but compared to ours it seems to me like a rich, aristocratic, handsome child compared to a clever man of the world, who is neither so aristocratic, rich, nor hand-

Palladio. The Basilica, Vicenza, c 1546–1617

some, but knows better what he can achieve with the means at his disposal.

When, here on the spot, I contemplate the magnificent buildings erected by that man and see how they have been disfigured by people's narrow, base needs, how these designs were mostly beyond the abilities of the builders, how poorly these choice monuments to a lofty human spirit harmonize with the life of the rest of mankind, then it occurs to me that this after all is the way of the world. For one gets little thanks from people when one tries to exalt their inner urges, to give them a lofty concept of themselves,

Palladio. The Basilica, Vicenza

to make them feel the magnificence of a true, noble existence. But when one deceives the birds, tells them fairy tales, leads them along from day to day, debases them, then one is their man; and that is why the modern era delights in so many tasteless things. I do not say this to disparage these friends of mine, I am only saying that this is how they are, and one must not be surprised if everything is as it is.

It is impossible to describe how Palladio's basilica looks next to an old castle-like building bespeckled with dissimilar windows, which the great architect certainly imagined as being absent, tower and all, and in a curious way I have to steady myself; for here too, unfortunately, I find the very things I am fleeing side by side with those I am seeking.

~ Italian Journey, 21 SEPTEMBER, EVENING

Today I visited the palatial house called the Rotonda, which is located on a pleasant height about a half hour from the town. It is a square building which encloses a round salon lighted from above. One climbs up broad steps on all four sides and each time arrives at a vestibule formed of six Corinthian columns. Perhaps there has never been more extravagant architecture. The space occupied by the steps and vestibules is much greater than that of the house itself; for each individual side would make a suitable view of a temple. Inside it can be called habitable, but not comfortable. The salon is very beautifully proportioned, the other rooms also; but they would hardly meet the needs of an aristocratic family for a summer sojourn. On the other hand one can see it from all sides in the whole area, rising up most magnificently. There is great variety in the way its central mass together with the projecting columns moves before the spectator's eye as he walks around it.

And just as the building can be seen in its splendor from all points in the area, so too the view away from it is most pleasant. One sees the Bachiglione flowing, carrying ships down from Verona to the Brenta. At the same time one surveys the extensive possessions that Marchese Capra wanted to preserve intact within his family.

The inscriptions on the four gables sides, which together make a whole, surely deserve to be recorded:

Marcus Capra Gabrielis filius
qui aedes has
arctissimo primogeniturae gradui subjecit
una cum omnibus

Palladio. The Villa Rotonda or Almerico, Vicenza, begun 1565–1566

censibus agris vallibus et collibus
citra viam magnam
memoriae perpetuae mandans haec
dum sustinet ac abstinet.

The conclusion in particular is rather strange: a man who had so much wealth and willpower at his disposal still feels that he must endure and abstain. That can be learned with less expense.

⤳ *Italian Journey,* 22 SEPTEMBER

I've seen a few more buildings and my eye is starting to be well-trained, I now have the courage to tackle the mechanical aspects of the art. What I'm pleased about is that none of my old basic ideas are shifting and changing; everything is just getting more clearly defined, developing, and growing to meet me.

⤳ *Flight to Italy,* 27 SEPTEMBER

Once again I've had my botanical ideas splendidly confirmed. It will certainly come and I'm advancing even further. Only it's odd and sometimes it makes me afraid, that such an immense amount is as if pressing in on me that I can't fend off, so that my existence is growing like a snowball, and sometimes it feels like my head can't grasp it or stand it, and yet it's all developing from within and I can't live if that doesn't happen.

⌒ *Italian Journey,* PADUA, 27 SEPTEMBER

At last I have acquired the works of Palladio, to be sure not the original edition with woodcuts which I saw in Vicenza, but an exact copy, indeed a facsimile with copperplates put out by an excellent man, Smith, the former English consul in Venice. It must be granted to the English that they have known for a long time how to appreciate what is good and have a grandiose manner of displaying it.

In connection with this purchase I entered a bookstore, which in Italy has quite a characteristic appearance. All the books stand around unbound, and good company is found there all day long. Those secular clergymen, nobles, and artists who are to any degree connected with literature walk to and fro here. A person may request a book, look something up, read, and converse, as he pleases. Thus I found some half-dozen men standing together, all of whom looked around at me when I inquired about Palladio's works. While the owner of the store was searching for the book, they praised it and gave me information about the original and the copy, for they were very well-acquainted with the work itself and the merits of its author. Since they took me for an architect, they praised me for proceeding to this master's studies in preference to all others. They said that he provided more material for practical use and application than Vitruvius himself did, for he had thoroughly studied the ancients and antiquity and tried to adapt it to our requirements. I conversed for a long time with these friendly men, learned some more things about the city's noteworthy sights, and took my leave.

The university building alarmed me by all its solemnity. I was glad I did not have to study there. An academic situation as crowded as that is inconceivable, even to someone who, as a student at German universities, has experienced discomfort on lecture hall benches. The anatomical theatre especially is a model of how students can be squeezed together. The listeners are layered above one another in a high, sharply-tapering funnel. They look almost straight down at the narrow space where the table stands, on which no light falls, so that the teacher must demonstrate by lamplight. In contrast, the botanical garden is pleasant and bright. Many plants can stay outdoors even in the winter if they are set next to the walls or not far from them. In October the whole place is covered over, and then it is heated for a few months. It is agreeable and instructive to wander amidst vegetation that is foreign to us. We eventually think no more at all about plants we are accustomed to, like other long-familiar objects; and what is observation without thought? Here in this newly encountered diversity that idea of mine keeps gaining strength, namely, that perhaps all plant forms can be derived from one plant. Only in this way would it be possible truly to determine genera and species, which, it seems to me, has heretofore been done very arbitrarily. My botanical philosophy remains stuck on this point, and I do not yet see how to proceed. The depth and breadth of the problem seem equally great to me.

[...]

In the church of the Anchorites I saw pictures by Mantegna, one of the older painters, who astonishes me. What a sharp, sure immediacy is displayed in these pictures! It was from this altogether genuine quality of immediacy—by no means specious, with no false effects that speak only to the imagination, but a robust, pure, bright, detailed, scrupulous, circumscribed immedi-

acy, which at the same time had something stern, diligent, labori-
ous about it—that the subsequent artists proceeded, as I noticed
in Titian's pictures. And now the liveliness of their genius, the
energy of their nature, illuminated by the spirit of these predeces-
sors and invigorated by their strength, could climb higher and
ever higher, rise from the earth and bring forth heavenly but true
forms. It was thus that art developed after the barbarous times.

The audience room of the city hall, rightly named "Salone," with
the augmentative suffix, is a self-contained structure so enormous
that it cannot be imagined or even, shortly afterwards, clearly
remembered. Three hundred feet long, one hundred feet wide, and
one hundred feet high beneath the vaulted roof that covers its
whole length. These people are so accustomed to living in the open
air that the builders found a marketplace to roof over for them. And
there is no question that the huge arched-over space produces a
peculiar sensation. It is an enclosed infinity, more analogous to
man than the starry sky is. The latter draws us out of ourselves; the
former very gently presses us back into ourselves.

୶ *Italian Journey,* VENICE

So it was written on my page in the Book of Fate that in 1786,
on the twenty-eight of September, at five o'clock in the evening by
our reckoning, I should for the first time lay eyes on Venice, sail-
ing out of the Brenta into the lagoons, and soon thereafter enter
and visit this wonderful island city, this beaver republic. And so,
God be thanked, Venice too is no longer a mere word to me, a hol-
low name which has often made me uneasy, me, the mortal
enemy of verbal sounds.

When the first gondola approached the ship (this is done so that
passengers who are in a hurry may be taken to Venice more swiftly),
I remembered an early childhood toy I had not thought about for
perhaps twenty years. My father owned a pretty model gondola that
he had brought back; he prized it highly, and I felt very honoured

when I was actually allowed to play with it. The first prows of shiny iron plate, the black gondola cabins, all of that greeted me like an old acquaintance, and I revelled in a pleasant, long-forgotten childhood impression.

 Italian Journey, THE 29TH, MICHAELMAS, EVENING

So much has already been told and printed about Venice that instead of a detailed description I shall just give my personal impressions. What again claims my attention above all else is the populace, a great mass, a necessary, instinctive existence.

This race did not flee frivolously to these islands; it was not caprice that prompted subsequent settlers to unite with them; necessity taught them to seek their security in this most disadvantageous location, which later became so advantageous for them and made them wise when the whole northern world still lay captive in darkness; their increase, their riches, were a necessary result. Now their dwellings crowded together ever more closely, sand and swamp were replaced with rocks, the houses sought the air, like trees that stand close to each other, and had to gain in height what they lacked in width. Niggardly with every span of ground and compressed into narrow spaces from the very outset, they allowed the lanes no more breadth than was required for separating two opposite rows of houses and preserving scanty passageways for the citizen. Furthermore, water served as their streets, squares, and promenades. The Venetian had to become a new species of creature, just as Venice can only be compared with itself. The great serpentine canal is second to no other street in the world, and nothing can really match the expanse before St. Mark's square: I mean the great watery surface which on this side is embraced in a crescent shape by the main part of Venice. To the left across the water one sees the island of San Giorgio Maggiore, somewhat more to the right the Giudecca and its canal, still farther to the right the Dogana and the entrance to the Grand Canal,

Palladio. The Salute and The Redentore, Venice

where immediately several huge marble temples gleam at us. There, with a few strokes, are the chief objects that catch our eye when we step out from between the two columns of St. Mark's square. All the views and prospects have been engraved so often that anyone who likes prints can easily get a vivid idea of them.

[...]

⁓ *Italian Journey,* THE 29TH, MICHAELMAS, EVENING

[...]

After dinner, I first hastened to obtain a general impression and, without a companion, noting only the points of the compass, plunged into the labyrinth of the city, which, although thoroughly cut up by larger and smaller bridges. One cannot imagine the narrowness and density of the whole without having seen it. Usually the width of the lanes can be nearly or completely measured by stretching out one's arms; in the narrowest, a person walking with arms akimbo will hit against the walls with his elbows. There are indeed wider lanes, even an occasional little square, but everything can be called relatively narrow.

I easily found the Grand Canal and the Rialto, the principal bridge; it consists of a single arch of white marble. The view down from it is grand, the canal thickly dotted with boats that bring in all the necessities from the mainland and dock and unload chiefly here, in between them a swarm of gondolas. Especially today, it being Michaelmas, the view was lively and very beautiful; but in order to describe it to some degree I must give a few more details.

The two main sections of Venice, which are divided by the Grand Canal, are connected by a single bridge, the Rialto, but rowboats provide additional communication at specific crossing points. It looked very good today when well-dressed but black-veiled women, in large groups, had themselves rowed over to reach the church of the fêted archangel. I left the bridge and approached one of those crossing points to get a close look at the disembarking women. I found some very lovely faces and figures among them.

Having grown tired, I got into a gondola and left the narrow lanes. To enjoy the spectacle on the opposite side properly, I rode through the northern part of the Grand Canal, around the island of Santa Clara in the lagoons, into the canal of the Giudecca, up toward St. Mark's square, and was now suddenly a co-sovereign of the Adriatic Sea, like every Venetian when he reclines in his gondola. At this point I thought respectfully of my good father, whose greatest pleasure was to tell me about these things. Will I not do the same? Everything around me is estimable, a great, venerable accomplishment of collective human strength, a magnificent monument, not of a ruler, but of a people. And even if their lagoons are gradually filling up, evil vapors hover of the swamp, their trade is weakened, their power diminished, yet the whole structure and substance of this republic will not for a moment seem less honourable to the observer. It is succumbing to time, like everything that has a visible existence.

Palladio. St. Georgio Maggiore, Venice, c 1564-1580. Façade 1607-1611

Flight to Italy, 1ST OCTOBER

Apart from some hard work on *Iphigenie,* I've spent most of my time on Palladio, and can't put him down.

[…]

In Verona and Vicenza I saw what I could for myself; it was only in Padua I found the book now I'm studying it and the scales are falling from my eyes, the mists are dissolving and I understand the objects I see. Simply as a book it's a great work. And what a man he was! My love, how happy it makes me that I've devoted my life to what is true, as it's now such an easy transition to greatness, which is the highest purest point of truth.

The revolution that I foresaw and that is now going on within me is the same as has happened to every artist who for a long time was diligently true to nature and now beheld the remains of the great ancient spirit, his soul swelled within him and he felt a kind of inward transfiguration of himself, a feeling of freer life, higher existence, lightness and grace.

I wish to God I could keep my *Iphigenie* another half-year, people would be able to sense the southern climate in her even more.

⟿ *Flight to Italy,* 5TH OCTOBER

With architecture things are getting better by the day. If you jump in, you learn to swim. I've now got a rational grasp of the orders of columns and can mostly say why they're as they are too. I can now keep the dimensions and relationships in my mind, whereas I found them incomprehensible and impossible to retain when they were merely something to be learned by heart.

[...]

The way I'm writing all this down for you, I won't have much left for when I'm back. I can definitely say I haven't had a single thought that seemed to me worth anything without at least giving some hint of it in a few words. As it's not yet time for the theatre, a word about Palladio following on from yesterday's. In the works he carried out, especially the churches, I've seen a lot to criticize alongside the very greatest things, so that it felt as if he was standing there beside me and saying: this and this I did against my will, but I did it because that was the only way I could get anywhere near my ideal in these circumstances.

It seems to me that when looking at a square, a dimension of height or breadth, a pre-existing church, an older house for which he was supposed to add façades, he simply thought: how are you going to get this whole thing into the grandest form, you may have to botch this or that detail, here or there it will produce an incongruity, but never mind, the whole will have great style and you'll get pleasure from working on it, and so he put up the great picture he had in his mind even in places where it didn't quite fit, where he had to fragment or mutilate it. That's why I so value the wing in the *Carità*, because there he was doing exactly what he wanted. If it were finished, then perhaps there would now be no more perfect piece of architecture in existence in the world.

I'm getting an increasingly clear picture of all this (i.e. the way he thought and the way he worked) as I read more of his works, or rather see how he treats the ancients. For he uses few words, but they are all weighty. It's the fourth book, on the Temples of Antiquity, that is a real guide to the way you should see Rome.

The really remarkable thing is the way other architects before and after him have chewed over these difficulties and the only solution they've found is a golden mediocrity. I'll grasp all that even better when I've got past the elementary classes.

⌒⌣   *Italian Journey,* 6TH OCTOBER

In Palladio's finished works, especially the churches, I have found many objectionable features side by side with the choicest ones. When I meditated about how much justice or injustice I was doing to this extraordinary man, I felt as if he were standing beside me and saying: "That and that I did unwillingly, but did it nevertheless, because under the existing circumstances it was the only way in which I could come very close to my most sublime idea."

After much thought on the subject, it seems to me that when he contemplated the height and width of an already existing church or an older house, for which he was supposed to erect façades, he would just reflect, "How can you give the greatest form to these spaces? In the details, as necessity dictates, you will have to displace or both something, there or there something unsuitable will result, but never mind, the thing as a whole will have a sublime style and you will be satisfied with your work."

And so the magnificent vision he cherished in his soul was applied even where it was not quite suitable, where he was forced to compress and stunt it in its details.

Palladio. Palazzo Chiericati, Vicenza c.1550–1557

The wing in the Carità, on the contrary, must necessarily be of very great value to us because there the artist had a free hand and was allowed to carry out his intentions unconditionally. If the monastery had been completed, it would probably be the most perfect work of architecture in the whole modern world.

How he thought and worked becomes increasingly clear to me as I read on in his book and observe how he deals with the ancients. For although he uses very few words, they are all weighty. The fourth volume, which describes the ancient temples, is the right introduction for anyone who wishes to view the ancient remains with understanding.

A word before I go to the opera.

[…]

St. Giorgio a fine monument to Palladio, although in this case he was following not so much his own genius as the genius of place.

[…]

Carità. I found an indication in Palladio's Works that what he intended here was a building to imitate the private dwellings of Antiquity, the upper classes naturally. I hurried off there avid to see it but alas hardly a tenth of it is executed. Yet even this part worthy of his divine genius. A perfection in the design and a meticulousness in the execution such as I hadn't previously come across. In the mechanical aspects too, as the greater part was put up in brick (of which it's true I've seen other examples) a fine precision. I did some drawing after Palladio today and want to assimilate him at the deepest level.

Il Redentore. A beautiful and grandiose work of Palladio's. The façade much more praiseworthy than the one on St. Giorgio. These are works that have been engraved; we can talk about them. Just one general word. Palladio had absorbed so much of the existence of the ancients and felt the littleness and narrowness of the time into which he'd been born, like a great man who won't resign himself but sets out as far as possible to reshape the rest of his own noble conceptions. Thus he was not happy, so I infer from a mild phrase in his book, with the way people went on building Christian churches in the old basilica form, he tried to make his churches more like ancient temples. That led to some features that don't quite fit, which I think he managed to integrate in the case of the Redentore, but are too obtrusive in St. Giorgio.

Palladio. The Redentore, Venice, c1576-1580

Flight to Italy, 4TH OCTOBER

[...]

The Farsetti house has a precious collection of casts of the best pieces from Antiquity.

[...]

Also some very fine busts. I just feel even now how far behind I am in my knowledge of these things, still, it will come with a rush, at least I know the way. Palladio has shown me the way to this and to all of art and all of life. That perhaps sounds a bit odd, but yet it's not as paradoxical as when the sight of a pewter dish gave Jacob Böhme illumination about the whole universe.

~~⤳ *Italian Journey*, 8TH OCTOBER

At the seaside I have also found various plants whose similar character has led me to a better understanding of their nature. All of them are both lump and rigid, juicy and tough, and evidently it is the ancient salt of the sandy soil, and even more so the salty air, that give them these qualities; they are brimming with juices like water plants, they are firm and tough like mountain plants; in cases where the ends of the leaves have a tendency to become prickly, like thistles, these prickles are extremely pointed and strong. I found a cluster of such leaves, which seemed to me like our harmless coltsfoot, but armed here with sharp weapons, and the leaf was like leather, also the seedpods and stems, everything plump and fat. I am taking along seeds and some leaves preserved in brine (*Eryngium maritimum*).

The fish market and the endless number of marine products give me much pleasure; I often go over there and inspect those unlucky creatures that have been snatched out of their home in the sea.

~~⤳ *Italian Journey*, 12TH OCTOBER

After I have, in conclusion, gone through my journal and inserted little remarks from my notebook, the documents shall be referred to a higher court, namely sent to my friends for their judgement. I have already found much in these pages that I could state more explicitly, amplify, and improve; but let them stand as a monument to first impressions, which we continue to delight in and treasure, even if they are not always true. If only I could send my friends a breath of this easier kind of life! Indeed the Italians have only a dim notion of the ultramontane, and to me too the other side of the Alps now seems dark; but friendly figures keep beckoning from the mist. Only the climate would tempt me to give preference to these regions over those; for birth and custom are strong ties. I would not care to live here or any other place where I would be idle; but at the moment I am very much occupied with new experiences. The architecture rises up out of its grave like an ancient ghost and bids me study its principles like the rules of a dead language, not so that I can practice it or enjoy it as something living, but only that I may, with a quiet spirit, honour the venerable, forever departed existence of past ages. Since Palladio relates everything to Vitruvius, I have procured the Galiani edition for myself; but this folio volume weighs down my luggage as heavily as the study of it does my brain. Palladio, through his words and works, his manner of thought and action, has already brought Vitruvius closer to me and interpreted him better than the Italian translation can do. Vitruvius is not very easy to read; the book in itself is obscurely written and requires judicious study. Nevertheless I am glancing through it, and am left with many a valuable impression. Or better: I read it like a breviary, more out of piety than for instruction. Night is already falling earlier, which gives me more time for reading and writing.

God be thanked, how dear to me again is everything I have esteemed since childhood! How happy I am that I dare again to approach the ancient writers! For now I may say it, may confess my morbid foolishness. For some years I could not look at any Latin author or contemplate anything that revived in me the image of Italy. If it chanced to happen, I would suffer the most dreadful pain.

[...]

If I had not made the resolution I am now carrying out I would simply have perished, so ripe had the desire become in my heart to see these sights with my own eyes. Historical knowledge was of no benefit to me, for while the things stood there only a hand's breath away, I was separated from them by an impenetrable wall. Even now I really do not feel that I am seeing the objects for the first time, but as if I were seeing them again.

Just a word! If someone could only tell the story of some granite column which was first cut in Egypt as part of a temple at Memphis, then dragged off to Alexandria, later made the journey to Rome, was there toppled and erected again after some centuries in honour of a different god. O my love, what is the highpoint of all human activity? To me as an artist what is most precious is that it gives the artist a chance to show what is in him and to bring unknown harmonies up from the depth of existence into the light of day.

Two human beings whom I think of as great in an absolute sense I have now got to know more closely, Palladio and Raphael. There wasn't a hair's breadth of arbitrariness in their work, what makes them so great is that they knew the limits and laws of their art in the highest degree and moved within them and practised them with complete ease.

The following chapter, which is more directly connected with what Goethe presents in THE METAMORPHOSIS OF PLANTS about the insights he gained in Padua in the Botanic Gardens, was intended to be part of the original essay. We were advised against including that material in an essay on art history.

The irony was, of course, that the whole essay is, in a sense, about the divide that has opened up since Goethe's time between the arts and sciences—well, certainly between the academic departments representing the arts and the sciences. This absurd situation is injurious to both camps. Therefore, we are grateful that this publication gives us the opportunity to venture into Goethe's Plant Studies.

....

Acanthus Flowering Plant

Goethe's Fan Palm
Botanical Gardens, Padua

Appendix II

The Mysterious Architecture of
the Formative Forces

AN OBVIOUS CONNECTION between Palladio's works on architecture and Goethe's scientific writings is the approach that is followed. Palladio of course, follows Vitruvius as a model, and the content of their books is more obviously related by subject. Nevertheless the same procedure is followed by Goethe too in his major works on plants and later on color. Perhaps he felt that to show the "mysterious architecture of the formative process"[1] of nature he could follow the method of Palladio in explaining the architecture of human creation.

A cursory look indicates that all are divided into short sections—In Goethe: Introduction, Of the Seed Leaves, Development of the Stem Leaves, etc.; in Vitruvius, Section IV, Book 1: Introduction, Origins of the Three Orders, Ornaments of the Orders, etc.; and Palladio's begins: Of the several partics, etc., of Timber, Of Stones, etc.

In all cases the topic of study—Parts of the Plant, Nature of the Columnar Orders, Material used in Building—is treated in an ordered and analytic way, taking each unit and, as it were, placing one next to the other, then gradually building up.

---

1. See p32.

In itself, this is an architectural style of writing, as Douglas Miller notes in regard to Goethe's work on color in his introduction to *Goethe: Scientific Studies.*

> The architecture of *Theory of Colour* is extraordinarily refined, beginning with the momentary experience of colour in the human eye, then moving to the transitory creation of colour through colourless media (such as prisms), and finally to the permanent colours found in inorganic and organic objects. The capstone of his discussion, however, is the section on the sensory-moral effects of colour where he describes the intensified sensory response with its moral and even mystical dimensions. Each of these major parts has a similar inner development of its own, with clearly marked transitional sections to guide the reader from one type of phenomena to the next; we are led at every step to deepen our insight into nature and its underlying ideal if we can muster the imaginative activity demanded by the phenomena. [2]

It is not just a case of naming parts and then putting parts together, but each is presented in its relationship to the whole. Palladio and Vitruvius refer to this as the principle of "euritmia." In the plant the "gesture" may open out in one particular part, but can be found working formatively in the whole plant.

Although there is no judgement made as regards one part being better than another, of one columnar order being better than another, there is a clear moral approach taken. The language used expresses this in that it is qualitative as much as quantitative. For example:

Vitruvius, Book III p. 82: "without detracting at all from the general effect...."

---

2. Goethe, *Scientific Studies*, Volume 12 of the Suhrkamp Collected Works Edition, pXV.

Goethe, paragraph 106:[3] "… nature usually stops the growth processes at the flower and closes the account there, so to speak; nature precludes the possibility of growth in endless stages, for it wants to hasten towards its goal by forming seeds."

Palladio, Book II, Chapter X: "These halls must have been of an admirable magnificence, as well by reason of the ornament of the columns, as also for its height; because the soffit lay over the cornice of the second order, and must have been very commodious when festivals and entertainments were made there."

These examples were chosen at random and many others could be presented. They were not added on to moralize about how we should live or to anthropomorphize about how plants should behave. Their tone is rather an expression of the way these writers think about things, that they present their subject in relation to the human being who is above all a moral being.

Implicit in nature is a moral quality which in man is made conscious. This moral quality is apparent too in Darwin, although he presents nature with all the moral qualities of "the survival of the fittest." Consider this as the working principle of nature and the human being and compare it with Goethe's view of the world which he presents in his essay on *Wincklemann and his Age*.

When man's nature functions soundly as a whole, when he feels that the world of which he is part is a huge, beautiful, admirable and worthy whole, when this harmony gives him pure and uninhibited delight, then the universe, if it were capable of emotion, would rejoice at having reached its goal and admire the crowning glory of its own evolution. For, what purpose would those countless suns and planets and

---

3. Ibid., p94.

moons serve, those stars and milky ways, comets and nebulae, those created and evolving worlds, if a happy human being did not ultimately emerge to enjoy existence?[4]

The nodal leaves do not consciously "faithfully accompany the floret"[5] but Goethe speaks of this in moral terms just as he speaks of a process of "refinement and heightening" (in German, "Steigerung") going on in the plant.

In a building, the moral quality is put there by the architect. The halls are designed to have an admirable magnificence. Palladio is recognizing a quality that such buildings have. Again though, it is a relationship to the human being. Here we must make a fine distinction between recognizing the moral quality that is in something and judging whether one likes it or not. Of course in practice these are often done at the same time, though inclining more towards one or the other. Thus in Vitruvius "without detracting" is more judgmental and "the dignity of the whole" is more a recognition of its moral quality.

I am more concerned in this with the latter, which seems to me to form a kind of moral intuition about things. It is more obvious to exercise moral intuition with regard to architecture in order to understand what the architect has created. That the Rotonda, Basilica, and Redentore are different kinds of buildings is easy to intuit. However differentiating the Palazzo Chiericati from the Palazzo Valmarana requires a more exact intuition, one which must follow on from forming a clear imagination of the two. Goethe calls this "an exact sensory imagination," an imagination based first upon close observation and then recreating it with "the eye of the spirit." The moral quality, I would suggest, inheres in the intuition rather than the imagination since it is at that stage important not to make judgements and as noted earlier, it is difficult to discriminate between one's subjective liking or disliking

---

4. Goethe, *Essays on Art*, p101.
5. Goethe, *Metamorphosis of Plants*, paragraph 99.

and recognizing the moral quality in something. The distinction Goethe makes in his "Empirical Observation and Science"[6] between the empirical phenomenon, the scientific phenomenon, and the pure phenomenon would represent a similar distinction. The "observation" of the pure phenomenon is a moral intuition where one perceives the moral quality of the phenomenon.

In the *Italian Journey* with reference to Palladio, Goethe talks of "the great idea" he carried around with him. Thus, as we have mentioned, Palladio felt able to make reconstructions of ancient temples from the ruins that were left, even down to the detail of the decoration of which nothing remained, e.g., Book IV, Chapter XXVII on the temples of Pola.

In a similar way Goethe, after having experienced the plant archetype in Sicily, says that he would be able to invent plants that were true to nature: even though such plants did not exist, it would be possible for them to exist. Here we again touch upon a moral difficulty for the modern reader.

Nature is spoken of here as it is elsewhere as creative. One can intuit this creative process as one can intuit the imaginative process in an artist, with the distinction that the former is instinctive, the latter conscious (to a greater or lesser extent).

It ascribes to nature, not necessarily personality but moral being. How much natural selection based on a survival ethic can explain artistic and natural creative activity is a topic of debate today. It makes one cautious of ascribing moral being to nature oneself, but not of asserting that Goethe did, whether one agrees with him or not.

In Padua Goethe picked up a copy of Palladio's *Four Books*. He presumably must have looked through his new acquisition. Quite soon after this he is recording in his diary how during his visit to the botanical garden the question as to how to bring order to the study of plants has been occupying him. Perhaps a

---

6. Goethe, *Scientific Writings*, p25.

feeling that he could use Palladio's *Four Books* as a model was reinforced by his later acquisition and study of Vitruvius in Venice.

Just as Palladio has ordered the study of architecture, so perhaps might he order the study of plants. This thought was to come to fruition in Sicily in the public gardens in Palermo where the plant archetype swam "into his ken" for the first time; the seeing and the thinking came together as a moral intuition in a moment of knowing: "he discovers the unknown."[7]

The conversation with Schiller described in *Fortunate Encounter*[8] starts when Goethe asserts to him that there might be another way of approaching the study of plants than the dry, analytical approach of the lecture they have heard. It is this other approach that Goethe presents as his experience in Padua as part of his *Italian Journey* and in his other botanical writings.

In *The Metamorphosis of Plants* Goethe mentions "the date palm" which is clearly referred to in other essays as being one of the plants that caught his attention in the Botanic Gardens in Padua. The reference in section 20 makes it clear that the insight he gained from it was to do with how the variety of leaf form comes about.

If, as he asserts, the whole is contained in every part, even the smallest, then it seems probable that such a moment of insight as this clearly was, would be a first recognition of the plant archetype without actually seeing it. In the same way, a knowledgeable gardener can recognize from the first proper leaves, what the rest of the plant will be. These are quite distinct from the cotyledons (seed leaves) which "often appear unformed, filled with a crude material and as thick as they are broad."[9]

In paragraph 18 he adds:

---

7. Ibid. p25.
8. Ibid. p18ff.
9. Goethe, *Metamorphosis of Plants*, paragraph 12, *Scientific Studies*, p77.

... even the most leaflike cotyledons are always rather unde-
veloped in comparison to the later leaves of the stem. Their
periphery is quite uniform, and we are as little able to detect
traces of serration there as we are to find hairs on their sur-
faces, or other vessels' peculiar to more developed leaves.

They are as he asserts here "undeveloped" and take on form as
the leaf develops. Goethe then speaks about leaf veining and how
this is connected with the development of form in the leaf. This is
known as "anastomosis," i.e. the network of veins in a leaf.

(20) But further development spreads inexorably from node
to node through the leaf: the central rib lengthens, and the
side ribs along it reach more or less to the edges. These vari-
ous relationships between the ribs are the principal cause of
the manifold leaf forms. The leaves now appear serrated,
deeply notched, or composed of many small leaves (in
which case they take the shape of small, perfect branches).
The date palm presents a striking example of such successive
and pronounced differentiation in the most simple leaf
form. In a sequence of several leaves, the central rib
advances, the simple fanlike leaf is torn apart, divided, and a
highly complex leaf is developed which rivals a branch.[10]

Here is the reference to "the date palm" in the gardens in
Padua—it presents a striking example of the development of leaf
form. He then goes on to describe exactly what happens in the leaf
of the palm, what he saw there and what you can still see if you go
there today and look at the "Palma di Goethe." One could not put
it more precisely or succinctly. If you compare the manner of
description of this with that of Palladio there does seem a clear
connection of style. He says of Palladio that there is nothing "arbi-
trary" in his work.

---

10. *Scientific Studies*, p78-9.

A few paragraphs further on we find a passage which echoes much of what has already been discussed in this essay.

(24) Although the leaves owe their initial nourishment mainly to the more or less modified watery parts which they draw from the stem, they are indebted to the light and air for the major part of their development and refinement. We found almost no structure and form, or only a coarse one, in those cotyledons produced within the closed seed covering and bloated, as it were, with a crude sap. The leaves of underwater plants likewise show a coarser structure than those of plants exposed to the open air; in fact, a plant growing in low-lying, damp spots will even develop smoother and less refined leaves than it will when transplanted to higher areas, where it will produce rough, hairy, more finely detailed leaves.[11]

We have encountered this comparison before on the slopes of the Brenner and in Venice where he refers to the effect of growing in a high altitude or low down, in dry air or near the water. A plant growing in "low-lying damp places" will even develop smoother and less refined leaves. They will therefore be more like cotyledons.[12]

Later on in his description of the Calyx we find something which presents a polarity to the unformed calyx where several "fully formed leaves" are gathered around a central axis, the leaves often undergoing a modification of the form.

How then does this variety of leaf forms come about?

It is through the forming of veins. If you look at those of the fan palm, you will see that they are like strong straight lines. When the leaf breaks up into leaflets it follows the straight lines of the veins. If you look at any leaf you will see a variety of veins. The

---

11. Ibid. p79.
12. This idea is followed through by Grohman in *The Plant.*

strong straight ones invariably lead to points on the outer surface circumference of the leaf. The broken rounded veins invariably echo the round parts on the edges of the leaf. This indication can be seen in several drawings of plants by Goethe, as well as drawings by Kniep who accompanied Goethe to Sicily.

It is a sense-perceptible fact that the variety of leaf forms owes its design to the interaction of this basic polarity, which on the circumference of the leaf is represented by curved forms and points, and in the anastomosis, the veining of the leaf is represented by straight lines and broken lines.

Although as a text it was unknown to Goethe, this polarity between broken and straight lines is fundamental to the ancient system of wisdom and divination contained in the "I Ching" or "Book of Changes."[13] In that system the hexagrams are represented by broken lines and straight lines, e.g.

```
 ─────────        ──   ──
 ──    ──         ─────────
 ─────────   or   ──   ──
 ─────────        ──   ──
 ──    ──         ─────────
 ─────────        ──   ──
```

There are 64 possibilities.

The "basic polarity" Goethe talks about in his note quoted on page 33 is known in this Taoist system as Yin and Yang. This thought goes back several thousand years. We have mentioned how in the plant this manifests in a sequential expansion from seed to leaf, and contraction from leaf to calyx, and so on expanding to the flower, contracting to the flowering parts, expanding to the fruit, and finally contracting to the seed. We have pointed now to another polarity in the anastomosis, the network of veins in the leaf between the long straight veins and the broken curved ones.

---

13. Alice Raphael in *Goethe's Parable* does suggest however that Goethe had some knowledge of Chinese Taoist thought and was responsive to it. See pIX.

He has related the former sequence—from cotyledon to leaf to calyx to flower—to such conditions as wet and dry, cold or warm. In paragraph 24 Goethe says: "…the leaves owe their initial nourishment to the more or less modified watery parts which they draw from the stem." He says further that the variety of leaf form comes about in connection with something else: "They are indebted to the light and air for the major part of their development and retirement."

Elsewhere in a more pointed remark he refers to the veins of the leaf as channels, not of blood like human veins, or of water like the canals in Venice, but of "light and air." On many leaves you can clearly see an indentation on the surface of the leaf. They really are miniature channels. The leaf form is created by the working of light and air though the veins of the plant. Further, when one regards the beauty of this veining process on any plant, one really does feel that nature is creative like the artist, and that the artist can learn much from nature. At the end of the *Chymical Wedding of Christian Rosenkreuz* one of the "mottos" given to Christian Rosenkreuz is "Art is the Priestess of Nature."

If I may return to the bookshop in Padua where I started this sequence of thoughts, I suggested that it may have been that the friendly Padovans who praised his choice of book and extolled the value of Palladio's writing may have pointed out to him that Palladio mentions Padua in his books. They may even have found the extract for him. Alternatively, it may have been in the quietness of his room that Goethe came across the reference to Padua himself.

In connection with his experiences of the palm tree in Padua, Goethe points to the way that light and air "develop and refine" the leaf. Palladio's buildings are masterpieces of light and air, as anyone who has walked around one can testify. The exteriors of his buildings are built to be seen in relationship to the light, most obviously the Villa Rotonda with the light and shadow moving around its different façades. Peter Murray, writing on the Basilica notes, "The architectural effect is dependent on the play of light and shade in the arches themselves, opposed to the solid masonry, but it is due also to the great subtlety of the actual shapes of the openings and the architectural elements."[14] Palladio often mentions the importance of light and air to a building, but in his reference to Padua in the *Four Books* he talks about how the whole city is designed and laid out with regard to the light and air.

Whether or not Goethe realized it, the Italian word *piñata* is used for both "the plant" and "the ground plan of a building or place," as well as for a map of a town.

In his books Palladio writes about Padua in connection with the plan, the layout, the *piñata* and about the city. What moral, practical and artistic considerations should govern this? Goethe buys a copy of the work in Padua. In his botanical writings he speaks about an experience of great importance in connection with his plant studies in Padua. He comes to understand how the development and the refinement of leaf form are connected with the working of light and air on the plant.

One can follow this thought in various directions. For example, in Venice the streets, which in a certain sense correspond to the veins of the leaf, become channels of water. In the *Italian Journey* Goethe makes several remarks about the layout of the city and in particular how the watery element affects this. He is also interested in how the watery element affects the growth of plants when he visits the Lido in Venice.

Another line of thought is to consider how the basic polarity working to create the form of the leaf is made visible in the straight line and the curved line. In Vicenza Goethe has already written about a fundamental polarity to be seen in architecture, that between wall and column.

This echoes the polarity of straight line and curve, though it does so in three dimensions rather than two. The wall is essentially a straight line; certainly on the plan it appears so.[15]

---

14. Murray, P. *Architecture of the Italian Renaissance*. London: 1969, p212-3.
15. It would be pedantic to argue that some walls are curved.

The great variety of form—whether in leaf or building—comes about through this fundamental polarity. It can be clearly seen. You can consider how the rounded form of the cotyledon changes to the radiating lines focussed on a point which the calyx images, i.e., presents as an imagination, ready-made as it were. The leaf presents a multitude of variations on how to progress in sequence from one to the other, and so, similarly, does the creative polarity of column and wall, except in that case what is formed is a multitude of spaces, internal or external. The buildings of Palladio are beautiful works of art, but the space in them and around them is also impressive.

The plant archetype comes to expression as actual plant through this polarity of line and curve. Palladio brings "the great idea" he has in his mind to its various expressions through the contradiction of wall and column.

Goethe was looking for the ordering principle through which he could understand the various forms in which the plant came to expression. There seems to me to be a clear connection here between what he came to understand of "how Palladio worked" in creating his buildings and of how nature works in creating plant form.

In anticipation of where this leads, let me quote the art historian H. Wölfflin: "Certain passages of *The Metamorphosis of Plants* have exact parallels in the history of art."[16] However, the last word should be with Goethe: "Beauty is an archetypal phenomenon. While it never materializes as such, it sheds its glow over a thousand different manifestations of the creative spirit and is as multiform as Nature itself."[17]

---

16. F. Amrine et al (eds), *Goethe and the Sciences: A Reappraisal*, p138.
17. Quoted in Naydler, J. *Goethe on Science*, p107.

BIBLIOGRAPHY

Amrine, F., Zucker, F.j., and Wheeler, H. *Goethe and the Sciences: A Reappraisal.* Dordrecht, Holland: D. Reidel, 1987.

Bernd, C.a. Et Al. *Goethe Proceedings at University of California, Davis.* Columbia, South Carolina: 1984.

Bergstraesser, A. (Ed.) *Goethe and the Modern Age.* Chicago: 1950.

Bortoft, H. *Goethe's Scientific Consciousness.* Tunbridge Wells: 1986.

Boyle, N. *Goethe, The Poet and the Age: Volume 1, The Poetry of Desire.* Oxford: Oxford University Press, 1991.

Curl, J.s. *Art and Architecture of Freemasonry.* London: 1991.

Eck, Caroline Van. *Organicism in Nineteenth Century Architecture.* Amsterdam: 1994.

Eckermann, J.p. *Conversations with Goethe.* Translated by J. Oxenford. Everyman's Library, 1930.

Fenmel, G. (Ed.) *Designi di Goethe in Italia: Exhibition Catalogue.* Vicenza: 1977.

Fink, K. J. *Goethe's History of Science,* Cambridge University Press, 1991.

Goethe, J.w.v. *Botanical Writings.* Edited and translated by B. Mueller. University of Hawaii, 1952.

_____. *Conversations of German Refugees, Goethe Edition, Volume 10.* Edited by J.k. Brown, translated by K. Winston and J. Van Heurck in cooperation with J.k. Brown. New York: Suhrkamp, 1988.

_____. *Corpus der Goethezeichnungen.* 7 Volumes. Edited by G. Fenmel. Leipzig: 1958-73.

_____. *Essays in Art and Literature. Goethe Edition, Volume 3.* Edited by J. Geary, Translated by E. and E.h. Von Nardroff. New York: Suhrkamp, 1986.

_____. *The Flight to Italy—Diary and Selected Letters.* Translated by T.j. Reed. Oxford: Oxford University Press, 1999.

_____. *From My Life: Poetry and Truth. Goethe Edition, Volumes 4 and 5.* Edited by T.p. Saine and J.l. Sammons, translated by R.r. Heiter and T.p. Saine. New York: Suhrkamp, 1984.

_____. *Italian Journey.* Translated by W. H. Auden and E. Mayer. Penguin Classics, 1962.

_____. *Italian Journey. Goethe Edition, Volume 6.* Edited by T.p. Saine and J.l. Sammons, Translated by R.r. Heiter. New York: Suhrkamp, 1988.

_____. *Italienische Reise in Werke (Hamburger Ausgabe). Volume Xi.*

_____. *Scientific Studies. Goethe Edition, Volume 12.* Translated by D. Miller. New York: Suhrkamp, 1988.

_____. *Wilhelm Meister's Theatrical Mission.* Translated by G.a. Page. London: Heinemann, 1913.

Grey, R.d. *Goethe and Alchemy. Cambridge:* Cambridge University Press, 1952.

Grohmann, G. *The Plant (2 Volumes).* Stuttgart: 1988.

Hennig, J. *Goethe and the English Speaking World.* Berne: 1988.

Hoffmeister, G. Et Al. *Goethe in Italy.* Amsterdam: 1988.

Holberton, P. *Palladio's Villas.* John Murray, 1990.

Lagerlof, M.r. *Ideal Landscapes.* New Haven: Yale University Press, 1990.

Naydler, J. *Goethe on Science.* Edinburgh: Floris Books, 1996.

Palladio, A. *The Four Books of Architecture.* Translated by R. Taverner and R. Schofield. Massachusetts Institute of Technology, 1997.

Padovan, R. *Proportion.* London: E. & F.n. Spon and New York: Routledge, 1999.

Pevsner, N. *Goethe and Architecture.* In *Studies in Art, Architecture and Design 1, 1968.*

Robson-scott, G. *Goethe and the Visual Arts.* London: Birkbeck, 1967.

Rykwert, J. *The Architects of the Eighteenth Century.* Cambridge, Massachusetts and London: 1980.

Steiner, Rudolf. *Goethe's Science: Introductions to Goethe's Natural Scientific Works in Kurschner's Deutsche National Literature.* Collected and translated by W. Lindemann. Spring Valley, NY: Mercury Press, 1988.

_____. *The Temple Legend.* London: Rudolf Steiner Press, 1985.

Striebel, Andreas. *Goethe e Palladio.* In Caputo, F. and Maseiro, R., (Eds), *Neoclassico; la ragione, la memoria, una citta: Trieste.* Venezia: Marsilio, 1990.

Summerson, John. *The Classical Language of Architecture.* Thames and Hudson, 1963, Revised Ed., 1980.

Taverner, R. *Palladio and Palladianism.* Thames and Hudson, 1991.

West, T.m. *The History of Architecture in Italy. London:* University of London, 1968.

Wittkower, R. *Architectural Principles in the Age of Humanism.* Academy Editions, 1988.

David Lowe *Simon Sharp*

David Lowe and Simon Sharp have been working together for twenty-one years. One of their first projects was the re-creation of Goethe's *Italian Journey*. They have given many workshops and presentations about it in the US and UK, including The British Museum, the German Embassy, and at the Edinburgh Festival.

DAVID LOWE was born in Barnsley, Yorkshire, into a coal mining family. He went on to study philosophy and politics at Queens College, Oxford, and later took his MA in art history at Oxford Brooks. Increasingly, his time is taken up with lecturing and study groups in the US and UK. The weeds in his garden in Oxford grow progressively taller.

SIMON SHARP is a teacher of Art and Design. He is currently Director of the Leonardo Centre at Uppingham School in Rutland, England. He uses Goethe's approach to observation extensively in his teaching and practical demonstrations. Trained originally as a designer, Simon believes in mixing art and science in his innovative teaching programs. He spends much of his time drawing and painting architecture and landscape.